Thru Navajo Eyes
Bluff to Monument Valley, Utah

Teachings of the Land Series
Digital App and Book Project

Volume 1
2014

Content: Robert S. McPherson
Technology: Jared V. Berrett

Download the App: www.teachingsoftheland.com

Appreciation is expressed to the
San Juan County Commission for its support
of this project.

A WORD OF CAUTION: Travelers visiting sites in this book are to exercise extreme caution when viewing the land formations and when parking and or entering traffic. Suggested sites for stopping should be used only when traffic allows you to do it safely. Do not drive distracted. The authors and project creators are not responsible for the use of stopping and viewing sites or safety thereof.

ISBN 978-0-9914741-0-3

Copyright ©2014 by Four Corners Digital Design
Printed in United States of America

For additional copies or comments contact:
Four Corners Digital Design
info@fourcornersdigitaldesign.com

Teachings of the Land (TOTL) Series:
San Juan County, UT

This book is the first in a series of written publications accompanied by a digital application for tourists traveling through southeastern Utah. Its purpose is to make available specific historical and cultural information not readily accessible without extensive research. Those who have lived in this region for centuries have a broad base of understanding or "Teachings of the Land" that is shared within this and subsequent monographs. Travelers will be introduced to a fascinating history and a variety of cultural teachings as they visit specific sites where it occurred. Come enjoy a memorable, TOTL learning experience from the comfort of your car. Teachings of the Land is at your fingertips.

The Digital App is downloadable to personal digital devices providing highlights on demand in a friendly GPS enabled cross platform framework. By combining digital and print medium, information is communicated to a wider audience and meets the needs of modern travelers. The book provides more detail, more stories, and insight to the culture of the region while the digital App. provides additional rich media, directions, and site specific extras.

All sites listed in this volume are accessible via the main highway but please be aware that there are many treasures off the beaten path. If you want to explore the region by land or river in more depth, please contact Four Corners Adventures or Wild Rivers Expeditions who are proud supporters of this book.

Four Corners Digital Design
Print | Web | Video

Layout, Design, App & Web Development
by Four Corners Digital Design
Jared Berrett
Cassidy Tait
Talon Kartchner

CONTENTS

Preface		iii
Contents		v
Introduction		1
General Map		10
Stop 1	Twin Rocks	11
Stop 2	San Juan River	13
Stop 3	Mule Ear	17
Stop 4	Butler Wash	19
Stop 5	Comb Ridge	22
Stop 6	Comb Wash	37
Stop 7	Lime Ridge Snakes	39
Stop 8	Lime Ridge, Creek, Sugar Loaf	41
Stop 9	Valley of the Gods	44
Stop 10	Missing Sandstone Block	49
Stop 11	Water from the Pipe	50
Stop 12	Southern Tip of Cedar Mesa	51
Stop 13	Goosenecks	53
Stop 14	Navajo Blanket	54
Stop 15	Mexican Hat	57
Stop 16	San Juan Trading Post	62
Stop 17	Alhambra and Halchita	68
Stop 18	Bears Ears	71
Stop 19	White Tipped Mountain	77
Stop 20	Douglas Mesa	79
Stop 21	Eagle Mesa	83
Stop 22	Monument Valley	85
Trip Notes		90

Teachings of the Land Series

TOTL

Thru Navajo Eyes
A Brief Tour in Southeastern Utah

The Navajo people (Diné) have one of the most extensive and interesting religious and philosophical expressions concerning the land of any Native American tribe in the United States. The core of this understanding comes from a large number of stories or teachings (Dinéjí Na'nitin) that are sacred and explain the world as the People see it. This view is complex, based on stories having various interpretations dependent on local knowledge that teach different values. This seemingly endless source of understanding is often embedded in metaphors and teachings that guide moral behavior; indeed the land is an intense mnemonic device, or memory-jogger, that helps the informed to understand the important things of life. This land can be as didactic as a Bible verse or as implied as one of Aesop's Fables, yet applicable to many aspects of the human experience. By sharing these teachings, one is expected to become a better person, to understand the realities of life, and to live with respect on Mother Earth with her creatures.

    This book provides a very limited view—a mere slice of what fills the Navajo universe with what is often called sacred geography. For the traveler looking for a single coherent story with scholarly references, he or she will have to go elsewhere and explore the rich literature found in libraries and oral history collections. Rather, what one encounters here is an accompaniment for an hour-long drive—literally on US Highway 163 between Bluff and Monument Valley, Utah, and figuratively through a land imbued with powers and teachings that go back to the "palm of time" or creation of the world when the Holy People walked the land. Travelers will explore from their car twenty-two geographic features important to the Navajo for a variety of reasons stretching from the sacred to the profane, none of which are necessarily connected in a linear sense. Each site stands on its own as a place of teaching and reflection. While it is not possible to share all that exists about any single feature, enough context is provided and teachings shared that people can understand the depth and significance of what lies before them. Some sites will require more time and a greater background of understanding than others, but all provide a piece of the picture of what the land means to the Navajo practicing traditional culture.

Before starting, some general context and principles should be considered. The first is that the land is both a physical and spiritual creation. The Holy People (Diyin Dine'é) created first spiritually then physically the world and everything in it. They are a powerful group of gods, interested in making a world filled with meaning and instruction for the Earth Surface or Five Fingered Beings (humans). The Holy People used organizing principles that are found throughout their creation such as the availability of power; opposition in all things; paired beings; a male and female dichotomy; ever-present spiritual influences; connecting dialogue to spiritual forces through prayer and song; and land-based healing traditions made manifest in ceremonies with their accompanying natural materials. Each of these is explained briefly to reinforce the concept that the land is much more than just what the eye beholds.

In the beginning the Holy People, in their spiritual form, gathered together to discuss the creation to include humans and all other creatures. These were powerful beings—Talking God, Black God, First Man, First Woman, Hogan God—to name a few. They built the first sweat lodge, a place for planning, discussion, and prayer, where they talked about the future and arranged what would be best. For every sickness there would be a cure, for every problem an answer, for every evil, good. The challenge that the Five Fingered Beings faced was to align themselves on the side of right, but still be given the opportunity to choose the dark side. To know good, one must also experience evil. As the animals and humans encountered good and evil in the three or four worlds (depending upon the version of the creation story) below, there arose problems—jealousy, fighting, witchcraft, and murder. The gods destroyed each of the worlds beneath this one, yet some of the occupants were able to move above into the next world. Chastened and purified from their previous experience, the inhabitants met new and different creatures, interacted with them, but eventually fell into the same trap, doing things that were wrong. Again purification, travel to the next world, and similar experiences were accompanied by a growing sophistication of thought, language, and spiritual form.

In the world beneath this one, problems persisted when men and women argued then separated. Later they came back together, having established important rules to govern their relationships. More trouble, this time when Coyote, the trickster and powerful holy being, stole two babies belonging to Water Monster. She became so angry she flooded the world beneath, forcing the inhabitants to escape through a hollow reed into this, today's world, (Hajiinéí—Emergence Place in the Fourth/Fifth World). Following their arrival, the plants and animals went to their respective places to live, humans received their physical form, and the Holy People's plans went into effect. This simplified version of an extremely complex, lengthy story is filled with teachings central to ceremonial practices and daily life. Indeed it is the core explanation of why the world is physically structured as it is; why, where, and how plants grow as they do and the curative qualities they hold; the personality and power of animals; and why people act in certain ways.

This expansive story is added upon with further teachings as the Holy People and the Navajo experienced things in this world. All of this joins together, often being compared to a stalk of corn, to explain life. As with a seed rooted in the ground, the kernel gives life to the stalk that breaks through the surface and reaches toward the sky. Along the way there are leaves that branch off, representing experiences and stories that are sacred and provide the basis for additional healing ceremonies. As one gets to the top of the stalk there is corn pollen used for offerings and blessings. The Navajo word for this pollen is tádidíín, glossed in English as "holy knowledge or light" and is placed on the tongue when praying or scattered when given as an offering. If ingested it is comparable to the sacrament in Christian ideology and becomes part of the person. And like the stalk of corn, it helps one to reach to the sky, the home of the Creator (Yá'ałnii Niníyá—He Who Stands at the Center of the Universe), an individual not often discussed.

Fundamental to understanding these stories and for happiness in life is the concept of k'é or relationships. Whether one considers human interaction or that between man and animals or other creatures or between humans and both animate and inanimate objects (as science classifies things), there is a relationship. Unlike the scientific world with its rules and laws, the central core of being in the Navajo world revolves around two "things" and how they communicate and act toward each other. For humans the concept of k'é means right living, based on principles of love and stewardship—caring and protecting a positive relationship. This term connotes spiritual and interpersonal harmony bonded through love and respect. These feelings are not limited to humans, however, but include all of nature. This is not to suggest that trees are not cut down, plants plucked, animals killed for food, or the land used for man's purposes. The spirit in which these things are done is what is important. Killing a sheep, harvesting an herb, planting corn, and crossing a river are all performed with prayer and communication between the person and the place, activity, or thing. It is the maintenance of a peaceful, caring relationship between the two that is of primary concern.

Another operating principle concerning the land is that all things on it hold power that can both help and harm. As with electrical current, this power can be of great assistance to those who understand its origin and how to control it. For those who do not have this ability, an uncontrolled power can be harmful and should be avoided or else sickness and death may follow. Still, it is an important thing to know that supernatural (or more than ordinary) power is available for healing, protection, and instruction if a person, usually a medicine man, wishes to use it. Different objects, animals, plants, and geographic sites have various types and levels of power—some being more potent than others. This is not determined by size or particular characteristics but rather the teaching, event, or personality associated with it. By understanding its qualities, one knows how to interact and have those powers directed in a beneficial manner. For example, a horned toad plays an important role in a story where he protects a young boy. In Navajo thought, this "Grandfather," as he is addressed as a term of respect, can assist with protection, comfort, and help in times of danger, but must also be handled and cared for in specified ways.

Another principle is based on opposites and opposition. While Christianity stresses that two opposite forces, good and evil, are in continual struggle with each other, Navajo thought recognizes that there are opposites that are not necessarily contending one with the other. Rather, power in the Navajo universe is present so that an individual decides how it should be used. As with electricity—is it to be used to cook a meal and light a home or to shock, harm, or kill a person? It is up to the individual who knows how to control it to decide. Thus a physical site may be a place where both prayers for healing and actions for witchcraft can take place. The power is in the site; how it is used needs to be determined. There are places, however, that are only used for evil—the ant'į́įh bighan (literally "corpse poison house") for example, is where witchcraft is performed with a group of skinwalkers. This type of meeting place is designed for evil purposes only. On the other hand, the four sacred mountains—Blanca Peak, Mount Taylor, San Francisco Peaks, and Hesperus Mountain—exist to bless the Navajo, support ceremonies, bring prosperity to the reservation, and protect the people. These are sacred places that provide power for the individual as well as a group. Few things could be more positive.

A part can represent the whole. The Holy People understand that everyone cannot have everything and that representation is effective and necessary to bring elements together. With various powers vested in the landscape, the only way that medicine men and devoted practitioners can access this power is to have something that comes from and holds it. Thus the blessings of the four sacred mountains can be kept in the home in what is called a mountain soil bundle. This medicine bundle contains a small amount of earth from the peaks of the four sacred mountains, bringing blessings of wealth, prosperity, health, and protection to the home where it resides. As part of the Blessing Way teachings, this bundle is a powerful positive force in the daily life of the family. Another example of the part having the qualities of the whole is where a feather represents the power and ability of the bird from which it comes. An eagle feather that has not touched the ground but is plucked from the bird or taken from its nest is called a life feather (hiinááh bits'os) and can carry prayers and thoughts to the Holy People just as the eagle flies in the sky. This principle of a part as whole is fundamental in understanding how the tools of a medicine man combine to become a potent force for healing.

In the Navajo universe all elements, both animate and inanimate, are either male or female. Rivers, mountains, trees, rocks, clouds, and so forth have a sex. Things that are male are jagged, sharp, powerful, hard driving, associated with war and death, and have the strongest type of power when compared with that of the female whose powers are softer, nurturing, domestic, and more peaceful in nature. Thus a male rain is torrential, destructive, and culminates in a rampaging gully-washer. Female rains soak into the ground, are misty, peaceful storms that nurture crops and gently caress Mother Earth. Jagged multi-branched lightning is male, sheet lightning female. Even the human body, regardless of sex, has a male side (left) and a female side (right)—a pattern used in ceremonies when arrowheads (destruction, death, and protection from evil) are handled with the left hand, while pollen is handled with the right. Thus the eye, ear, nostril, lung, etc. on the left side is male, the corresponding element on the right female. Geologic formations often receive their sexual classification from the stories and events as well as their physical properties.

Since there is both a male and female, many objects have a counterpart that may be located elsewhere. Pairs and multiple pairs are common in the Navajo universe. For instance, the four sacred mountains already mentioned are paired—two male, two female, and work together to bless the Navajo people. One of the sites discussed later is Comb Ridge, whose mate is the Hogback located to the east of Shiprock, New Mexico; the Bears Ears viewed along the road you will travel has a counterpart in the Carrizo Mountains. Glimpses of Navajo Mountain to the west provide a view of the head of a female form whose body is Black Mesa, running east-west, and whose mate is formed by the Chuska Mountains, running north-south. The female holds a wool twining device (bee'adizí) which is the El Capitan rock formation in Monument Valley while the male holds a medicine pouch (jish) which is the Shiprock formation in northwestern New Mexico. Two additional points to be made here is that there are a number of different stories and teachings about the same sites, deriving from different ceremonial origin narratives. The second is to recognize that the Navajos have an expansive understanding of a vast geographic landscape. In a day before airplanes allowed people to fly above for a comprehensive view, these people connected elements of the land in combinations that show keen observation.

     With all of these powers, personalities, and perspectives, there needs to be a way of connecting to them. Prayers and songs are the means given by the Holy People to unlock this power through a spiritual form of communication. Just as each individual has a sacred name that is used only in ceremonies or for very special occasions, so to do plants, animals, and sites. It is their spiritual identity, not for everyday use; but when used, it must be done with deep respect. Prayers and songs are the means by which an Earth Surface Being addresses and asks for assistance. The language and how it is used is a gift from the Holy People to make this journey on Mother Earth meaningful and to remind the People of the origin of all power.

     There is both an inner (spirit) and outer (physical) form for everything. The "form that stands within" (bii'yitiin) is what communicates on a spiritual level. As one spirit (human) prays or addresses another (rock, river, animal, etc.) the words are transmitted in a spiritual form through the Holy

Wind (Níłch'i), which in many respects is comparable to the Holy Ghost in Christian teachings. This Holy Being, without physical shape, warns, informs, teaches, and protects those it is helping. Always truthful, it pervades the universe and carries the communication of those praying to those being prayed to. One must listen and obey as advice is given and help rendered, otherwise the person obtaining this assistance receives no more. Prayer and song are the means, hold the power, and unlock the door to assistance, but it is the Holy Wind that carries it to the one who requests it.

The above principles work together in a unified Navajo universe. While much of it concerns the spiritual and intangible side of things, the teachings are also very much rooted in the physical world. Narratives and ceremonies are tied to specific locations that identify where events occurred, why certain plants, rocks, or other physical objects are located where they are, and how best to approach them for assistance. For instance within a song or ceremony an event will start at one site, progress to another, where Holy People are encountered, go to another, and so forth, each of which may assist in the healing process and some of which a person might visit for assistance just as it was found the first time it happened at the time of creation. In simple terms, it becomes a ceremonial itinerary. There are often long strings of physical sites mentioned as the Holy People moved about the landscape. And it was not by chance that specific animals or plants are found in certain locations. The Holy People put them there so that the land, plants, animals, and people can live in harmony and work together to support each other in different locales. This mutual support is part of how the Holy People designed the world to be—harmonious (hózhǫ́), a state of being that man is also to achieve. While this term is often glossed as peaceful harmony, it is so much more. It is a balanced spiritual state achieved by living in complete compliance with the rules established by the Holy People. Few, if any, achieve this status in life, but it is the intended goal for which one strives.

The land, as part of this process, reflects this and many of the values discussed here. Navajos recognize that it is not a perfect world, just as few people live a perfect life, but there are physical reminders along the way as to what is important and how one should act. In that sense, the land is filled with mnemonic devices that teach of a spiritual reality intertwined with the physical world. What is presented here is for public consumption—exoteric—given with the intent to educate people about how power and place come together in the physical landscape. There are no songs and prayers, no sacred ceremonial knowledge, but only a general explanation as to why a location is important and what may occur there. The specific words, actions, and places—the esoteric practices of the medicine man and religious devotees—is not shared for the benefit of the people. Traditional elders gave this information with the intent that it would benefit future generations and provide an explanation of powerful practices that have served the Navajo people well over the years. Hopefully what is available to all is an understanding and appreciation for these teachings. Now let's start the journey and discover exactly what the land has to share through Navajo eyes.

Thru Navajo Eyes

Bluff to Monument Valley
General Area Map with Stops

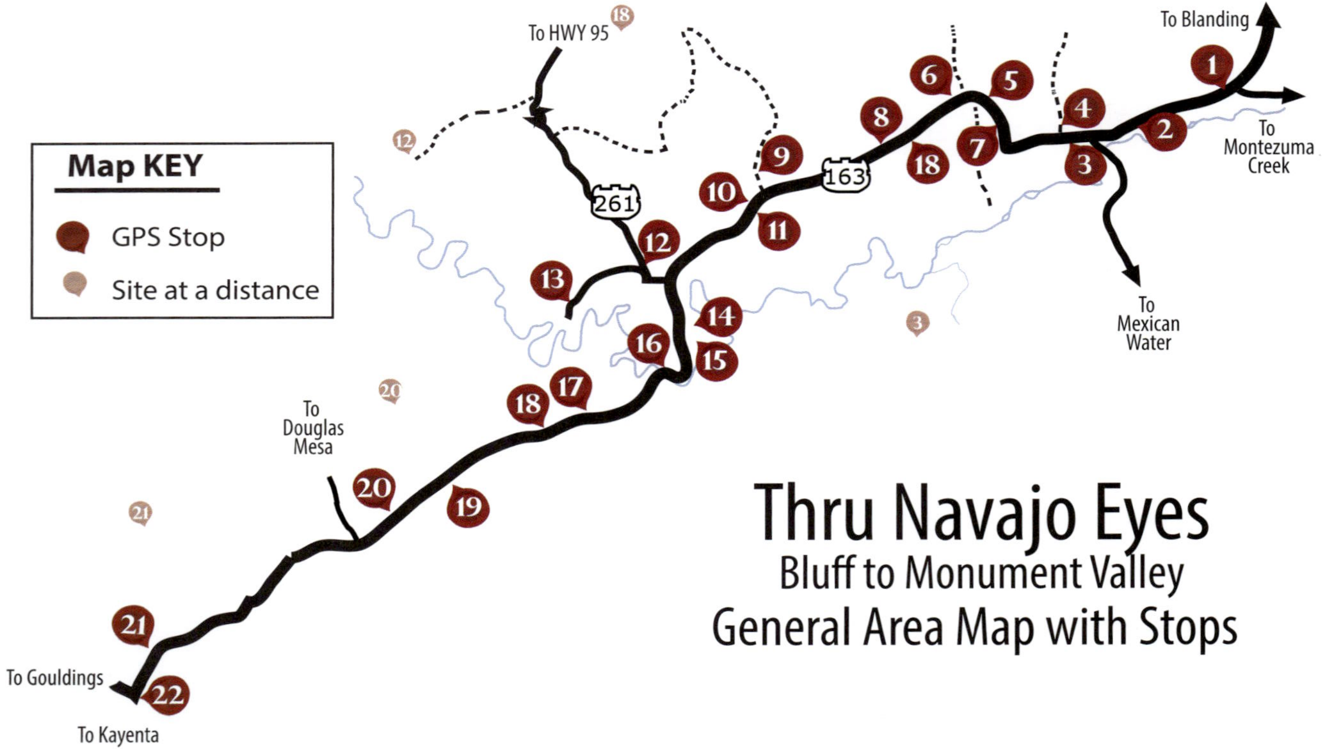

STOP 1
TWIN ROCKS

N37 17.184 W109 32.785

Stop One: Bluff—The Navajo Twins: Located on the northeast end of Bluff near the mouth of Cow Canyon rests the Navajo Twins comprised geologically of Bluff Sandstone. This landmark, to the Navajo, represents three things.

1. The name refers to the Hero Twins whose exploits are central to a number of healing ceremonies and whose behavior serves as an example of proper manhood. Monster Slayer (Naayéé Neizghání) and Born for Water (Tóbájíshchíní) journeyed to their father Sun Bearer (Jóhonaa'éí) in the sky where they received four types of arrows to destroy the monsters inhabiting the earth. After killing these evil creatures, they returned to the area of the San Juan River to assume a peaceful life. This rock formation is a reminder that these two deities with their extraordinary power are still available as Holy People to bless and protect the Navajo from evil influence, as guardians of the traditional way, as role models of bravery, and examples of the potency of prayer.

2. The birth of twins is a joyful event of which parents are justifiably proud. The Holy People have had a hand in the occurrence and so the offspring are said to be a "double divine gift" with every effort being made to preserve their lives through ceremonial observance. Children, in general, are a special gift, but to obtain twins, local Navajos in the past suggested that to lick the Navajo Twin Rock increased the possibility of a double birth.

3. This rock formation is also said to be two prayer sticks (k'eet'áán). Prayer sticks are colored according to the god whose power and assistance is desired and placed in different areas according to the deity being summoned. Some are simple in construction such as painted sticks while others have feathers, precious stones, arrowheads, and other objects attached as part of the offering. All are dedicated through prayer which remains with the k'eet'áán as part of its power to encourage a Holy Being to participate in a ceremony. The Navajo Twins are prayer sticks left by the Holy People, some say Monster Slayer, who value white shell, turquoise, abalone, jet, bluebird feathers, eagle and turkey down, mountain tobacco, and colors associated with the four directions. The layers on the lower part of this rock represent these objects so that when the Diné leave prayers and offerings in its vicinity, the Holy People assist. Around the corner from this rock to the north is a cove with an echo. Prayers petitioning Monster Slayer to protect servicemen going to war are amplified in their transmission by this echo.

STOP 2
SAN JUAN RIVER

N37 16.003 W109 36.640

Stop Two: San Juan River: Unlike the local knowledge concerning the Navajo Twins, the San Juan River figures heavily in many of the better-known tribal teachings. This 380-mile-long river begins high in the San Juan Mountains of southwestern Colorado and terminates today in Lake Powell, fed by the Colorado River. As with all physical entities discussed in this book, the river has a spirit or "form that stands within" (bii'yistiin). Like a human being, an object has a spirit that allows it to communicate, hold power, bless, harm, and protect those who come in contact with it. And as with everything in the universe, there is a male—the San Juan River—and a female—the Colorado River—that form a pair. Navajo land is bounded in the four directions by four sacred rivers (Rio Grande, Little Colorado, and Colorado) with San Juan being the river of the north. Historically, it has been the general dividing line between the Navajos (south) and Utes (north) as they struggled against each other during the eighteenth and nineteenth centuries. There are four key points in understanding what this river means to the Navajo.

1. The Diné believe that words and names hold power. Many creatures and objects have sacred names used only in ceremonies to invoke that power and are not for everyday use. Special names for the San Juan River include Old Age River (Sá Bitooh), Male Water (Tooh Biką'ii), Male with a Crooked Body (Biką'ii Bits'íís Nanooltł'iizhii), Decorated with Abalone

Shells (Bikáá' Hodiichı́łı́), and One with a Long Body (Bits'ı́ı́s Nineezı́). To some the sparkle on the surface represents the shine of lightning. It is a powerful river described as an old man with hair of white foam, as a snake wriggling through the desert, as a flash of lightning, and as a black club of protection that keeps invaders from Navajo lands.

  2. When a person comes to the river, he offers his corn pollen for a good journey and prosperity. "I will receive many things with this small amount of money or trading items." Before crossing the river, offerings are given to protect the traveler as he or she leaves the safety of Navajo land and enters into that of traditional enemies—Utes and Anglos. By leaving corn pollen or crushed precious stones, the traveler will have the power from the spirit-that-lives-within accompany him on his journey. That same spirit will help the person successfully achieve his goals and receive material assistance and wealth by following this practice. One woman recalled how Navajos prayed against their enemy. "The prayers were a tool to defeat evil or to hide behind for a safe journey." In addition to protection, rain, grass, and other good things come to the person who beseeches. Now that this practice of prayer for protection and assistance is no longer being performed, the land is dry, rain has decreased, accidents have increased, vegetation is short and withered, livestock is dwindling, drowning is prevalent, and harmony is scarce. When people paid respect to Navajo boundaries, life was safe and happy.

  3. Water, whether it falls from the sky or rests on the land, is vital to life and treated with respect, just as grandparents should be. This is the reason that water is referred to as a

grandparent or parent, because it provides for the People. In a ceremony, medicine men use it with yucca to cleanse before starting, during the ritual, and at its end. The residue of supernatural power that participants have been exposed to during the ceremony must be removed. This water is like food that has been used and is now returned to Mother Earth. Both earth and water are grandparents and addressed that way in prayer. In prayer, water is considered a female and so is treated as a living grandmother who holds lots of power. As with other family members, it blesses lives.

4. There are many stories that teach about the San Juan River and the power in it. For instance there are Holy People called Water Monsters who live within the depths of a body of water. Spinning, funnel-shaped whirls are entrances into their chambers where they drag victims. Outside of their homes may be found a pet, a "deep water horse" which serves as a guardian. Water Monsters have fine fur like an otter and horns like a buffalo, while their young may be spotted with various colors. Some people say they look more like a buffalo or hippopotamus. Other teachings tell of how Coyote the trickster stole two of Water Monster's babies, and so in revenge, the creature raised the level of water in the world beneath this one until people fled into today's world. When Coyote returned the stolen offspring, the waters subsided, but water now has an innate tendency towards anger and so can be very destructive, drowning people and flooding the land if not shown proper respect. Until the Navajo Dam in New Mexico harnessed the San Juan River, its flood waters, a raging flow of brown silt in the spring and torrential summer showers, was common.

Today, the San Juan River provides much needed irrigation water as well as recreational opportunities for hundreds of visitors each year. For a cool break from your trip, consider contacting Wild Rivers Expeditions in Bluff, Utah.

STOP 3
MULE EAR

N37 15.857 W109 38.512

Stop Three: Mule Ear: The Mule Ear diatreme, formed by an explosion of gasses in a volcanic pipe, is similar to many such features found throughout Navajo land—Alhambra (outside Mexican Hat/Halchita), El Capitan (Monument Valley), and Shiprock, New Mexico, for examples. These volcanic necks protrude because of eroded surface soil, standing in stark contrast to the lighter colored sandstone formations prominent throughout the region. Navajos see them as places of power.

    1. All of these rocks serve as sky supporters (yáya' nizíní—Those-who-stand-under-the-sky) that connect the heavens to the earth, having been put in place by the Holy People to separate and support the two. They also serve as places of communication, somewhat like a radio tower, that boost messages to the Holy People and so are good sites for prayers and offerings. In the same sense, some are viewed as prayer sticks.

    2. Mule Ear is known in Navajo as Designs-on-the-Rock or Decorated Rock (Tsénaashch'ąą'í). On one side at the top of the rock is a thin flat ridge where witching practices are said to be held. Another site nearby called Tsézhiin'íí'áhí or Standing Black Rock has strong powers used against people. The rock is witched and can cause starvation. As with many things in Navajo culture, power is neutral but present. Thus

blessings and prayers given at these formations, depending upon the intent of the person employing the rock's power, can either help or harm.

3. When the Holy People emerged from the world beneath this one, there was just a little bit of land surrounded by water at the place of Emergence, said to be in the area near Navajo Dam close to Farmington, New Mexico. The water needed to be drained to make room for the people. Four deities each took a large arrowhead and carved a trench through the earth allowing the water to flow in the four directions. These large rock points remain where they were used—one outside of Telluride, Colorado; another near Albuquerque, New Mexico; another near Moab, Utah; while the fourth is Decorated Rock. This arrowhead freed water that entered a system of rivers, including the San Juan and Colorado, eventually draining into the Gulf of California. This large arrowhead is left on the landscape to remind people of this event and, as an arrowhead—an object full of protective power—provides assistance to the People and their land. Evil fears an arrowhead and stays away. Next the gods stretched the earth, making it larger and pushing the oceans back. As you look at the rock formations that exist between Bluff and Monument Valley, you can see where the water used to exist before being released. As one elder said, speaking of the four points, "They are all related, just as we people are. We are one. They all live like we do altogether as one." Their power is there to assist the Diné. For those who know the traditional stories, this formation is also known as "Decorative Arrowhead."

STOP 4
BUTLER WASH

N37 15.857 W109 38.512

Stop Four: Butler Wash: Butler Wash, named after John Butler, who in 1879 was among the first in an advance party of Mormon settlers to explore the area, is famous for its Ancestral Puebloan (Anasazi) remains. Along the wash are a series of old Navajo campsites and collapsed hogans that testify that this was a favorite living area with grass for the sheep in the winter as well as a place to collect berries and sumac for basket weaving in the summer. The area of Butler Wash is rich with Navajo place names but there appears to be no single name for the wash that extends along the east side of Comb Ridge from the San Juan River to its head approximately twenty-two miles to the north.

1. Names upon the land, like signs, stores, and monuments in Anglo culture, describe what is important and give meaning to the area and directions for travel. A few for Butler Wash illustrate cultural values. For instance, "Under the Rock" provided shade for the sheep during hot summer weather; "Sumac Gathering Place" speaks for itself; "Small

Amount of Water Coming Out" was a welcomed resting spot for travelers; and "Whitehorse Lying Down"—a rock formation that takes some imagination—was a notable sign post. "The people used to say, 'The sun went down just when I reached the lying white horse' as they returned from visiting stores in Blanding."

    2. Butler Wash holds one of the richest concentrations of Anasazi dwellings and rock art panels between Bluff and Monument Valley. To the Navajo, contact with any of these remains was generally avoided except for an individual like a medicine man who understood how to control the spiritual power and prevent ghost sickness from attacking him. These Ancestral Puebloans were viewed as a gifted people who went astray, turned the sacred into the profane, and left behind a reminder that this is done only at one's peril. The Holy People who had blessed them with abilities similar to what Anglo people have today—control lightning (electricity), travel through supernatural means (cars and airplanes), make objects with power (from bullets to bombs)—saw that they did not say prayers, practiced evil things, and failed to leave offerings. They were destroyed by a number of means—wind, fire, loss of oxygen, hail, and whirling stones carried by the wind. Their story is one more mnemonic device that reminds the Navajo how to act and that excesses should be avoided.

River House Ruin

STOP 5
COMB RIDGE

N37 15.975 W109 40.458

Stop Five: Comb Ridge: This one-hundred-mile-long sandstone monocline is part of the Monument Upwarp and has served for centuries as a barrier to much of man's movements in the area. Navajo people have many teachings about the creation and use of this rock formation they call Rocks Standing Up (Tsé K'áán). As you travel through the actual formation, notice the old road that creeps between the rocks to the north. Blasted and opened for initial use in 1909, this road provided a challenge to both Anglo and Navajo travelers with their wooden wagons and old-fashioned automobiles.

First auto on old road to Bluff

    1. Big Snake/Snakes: Navajo mythology is replete with creatures and objects that provide protection. One of the most powerful in the creation story is Big Snake, a holy being who accompanied Changing Woman and other deities as they traveled about following the creation of this world. Big Snake and his earthly offspring, physical snakes of wide variety,

control significant power and are represented in Comb Ridge and its environs. Within a ten mile radius there lies a half dozen sites connected to Big Snake and his ability to protect; there are undoubtedly corresponding sites on other parts of the Reservation. Indeed, in ceremonial practice, one finds that there are one or more snakes that lie in the four directions, on each side of a sand painting to provide protection, as do other animals in different sand paintings. Some Navajo elders suggest that Comb Ridge is a frozen part of Big Snake, with its head pointing towards Blue Mountain. Known as Arrow Head Big Snake (Tł'iish K'aa') or Big Snake, this reptile is said to have been able to fly through the air. Breathing for this creature transpired through the alcoves found along the Ridge's side, the air passing in and out of these "vents." One Navajo elder explained, "Comb Ridge was not a rock when it was created, but was alive and moved around. The air pockets were made to give it air to breathe and to keep it alive. They are a part of its body like lungs through which it breathes. These air pockets were placed along its rib cage. When it was created, it was little, like a baby, then it grew. It became very big. All the rock formations were alive at one time." Falling rocks indicate the snake's "backbone" is injured, in part because of the highways that cut through it. The snake cannot heal itself and feels disrespected. "It is still alive and can hurt people because it is never given any offerings."

   A snake becoming a solid rock formation is not novel to Navajo thought. Monster Slayer traveled the land searching for evil creatures to kill to make the earth safe. When he reached the Chuska Mountains in New Mexico, he found two huge snakes. He walked along the back of one, then stepped from one to the other and went on. "Since that time, the two snakes lie there, having turned to stone." No exact location is specified for these two formations, but Comb Ridge (male) and the Hogback (female), its paired mate, lie within sight of the Chuska Mountains.

Some elders tell of a place near Comb Ridge called Place Where Water Collects (Tó Adinidahaskání). It is part of Big Snake, whose rattle is nearby. "They say that the tongue of the snake is at the other end, where it is smooth on the rock. Where the black rock ends, people say that is its hole. . . . The snake was returning to its hole, but was turned into stone before it reached home." Lime Ridge shares strong ties with Comb Ridge and its connection to Big Snake. One of another pair of snakes is visible as one drives through the blasted roadway passing through the Comb. (See Stop Seven: Lime Ridge Snakes) They reside within the ridge and are in concert with Big Snake and his power, providing protection in this part of Navajo land.

There are other places that hold similar power and are just as dangerous. A hole on the east side of El Capitan (Monument Valley) once was the home of Big or Endless Snake, a creature that traveled on the rainbow and wind. A medicine man from Navajo Mountain, described another home of this serpent as "a large hole with a bare entrance way. The vegetation around it is all dead or dying. People are forbidden to go near this place. This creature is capable of retrieving objects

Photo by Kay Shumway

from far away." Long ago a man living near Navajo Mountain lost his horse. He searched and searched until he found its tracks leading up to the creature's home; there were no tracks going out, only those where the snake had taken the man's horse. "They say this animal lures its prey from a distance of a mile, by way of electrical magnetic current or something like that." Other sites with similar phenomena are found in Kane Valley near the old VCA mine and Tsegi (Tséyi' meaning Canyon), west of Kayenta.

2. <u>Lightning and Arrowheads</u>: Closely associated with snakes are lightning and arrowheads. Looking along Comb Ridge in a panoramic side view, one sees serrated edges of rock that cut the sky. A particularly good view of this is when you reach the bottom of Comb Wash and look to the north along the escarpment. Traditionalists say that lightning lives in the points of the ridge or in pockets of rock along it. These pockets are also home to various types of wind. Lightning is said to look like a bird, whose dark green is the color of algae found in water. The electricity goes to the clouds and returns to earth just as a bird does. Comb Ridge is mentioned in ceremonial songs with reference made to illnesses caused by harmful things that come from the heavens.

  One woman described an experience related by her grandfather that took place in Mystery Valley, a part of Monument Valley and in close proximity to Comb Ridge. Lightning repeatedly struck a large oak brush- covered hill over the course of three days. The electricity became trapped in the roots of a large bush. The grandfather, a medicine man, "said it was a very small round object that was very shiny. It was covered with tiny lightning currents, like electricity, and made a sound each time it lifted the mound. Some people were observing it from a distance. Everyone was questioning what would happen to it and what they should do. 'I know what to do,' he replied. He prayed and prayed as he dressed like a Yé'ii Bicheii dancer (Holy Being in ceremony conducted during the winter] then walked up to the mound. He laid down a deer hide and spread it on the ground. The hide he used was not from a gun-or-weapon killed deer. . . . He then sprinkled some sacred corn pollen and ground white corn powder, yellow corn powder, mixed colored corn powder, and blue corn powder all over the spread deer hide on the ground. Then he prayed and talked to the lightning object, which later came out of the mound of roots and fell on the deer hide. He scrambled over and quickly wrapped it in the hide. Within the next few seconds, lightning struck the hide and took the object away. Many people there wanted the "shake offs" or residue from the captive lightning. Not until after medicine men performed a day-long ceremony was the powder given to those who wanted its protective power."

The Shooting Way ceremony cures people who have come in contact with lightning-struck objects and other illnesses. Lightning, arrows, and snakes are central imagery in this story about Monster Slayer and Born for Water, who traveled about making the earth safe for humans. Armed with various kinds of lightning received from Sun Bearer, the Twins set about protecting the People. At one point in the narrative, Monster Slayer visited the home of the Rattler People, out-performed their chief, and received different types of bows and arrows and sand paintings with cures. Soon after, he went to Striped Mountain, home of the Arrow Snake People, and then Coiled Mountain. No geographic location is specified, but a case could be made for the area around Comb Ridge as the latter site. Snakes, arrows, and lightning provide a complimentary mix threaded throughout this chant. The three are integrated as part of the Shooting Way philosophy "'concerning-the-shooting-of-objects-that-move-in-zigzags.' Lightning, snake, arrow, or indeed any one of many other names might have been chosen; all indicate what the chant stresses."

This ceremony "passed down through generations—only by the Holy Ones—is not a man–made ceremony" and requires special sand taken from Comb Ridge as do some other sand paintings. The sand does not come only from here, but it is one of a number of sites that provides materials. In addition to the complex practices of the Shooting Way, medicine men leave offerings at lightning struck trees and other places associated with it. Herbs and powerful songs, so powerful that they should never be sung while riding in a car or on a horse, are other ways of addressing lightning and thunder. When doing so, offerings and prayers are used, or else lightning will strike. "Lots of lightning prayers are said to calm it in some way. It is told to keep up in heaven as is the wind. This is why they are sung."

At the creation of this world, Decorated Rock, one of the four giant arrowheads previously mentioned, released water covering the earth. This point, in close association with Comb Ridge, becomes another protective symbol. One medicine woman believes that Comb Ridge, itself, is one of the four arrows that provide protection around the borders of Navajo land. A medicine man from Monument Valley and medicine woman from the Bluff area agree. They view Comb Ridge as an arrowhead that extends all the way to Blanding, but it also is a ridge made out of arrowheads lined in a row. The undulating serrations caused by its peaks are separate arrowheads, each providing individual and collective power and protection. The woman suggested it was made of flint, a word synonymous with arrowhead and identified with armor used by Monster Slayer.

    The belief for this extends back to the protective flint armor and arrows given to the Twins by Sun Bearer. Prior to returning to earth to kill monsters, the boys received arrows made of chain lightning, sheet lightning, sunbeams, and rainbows as well as protective clothing of flint. Thus prepared, they were ready to destroy the evil creatures, each of which had its own qualities and means of protection. Big God (Yé'iitsoh) wore armor which, once pierced by Monster Slayer's arrows, shattered and scattered. That is why flint is found strewn about the land. Then Monster Slayer said, "Let us gather those flint flakes. Our people can use them for knives. They can use them for arrowheads. They can cut with them and hunt with them."

    "Yes they can," replied Born for Water, "That way we can turn Yé'iittsoh's evil into something good."

    Arrowheads, knives, and other objects made of flint are synonymous with protection and safety.

    Another monster, Walking Rock (Tsé Naagáí), needed to be killed in a different way. He crushed those who came close. "Monster Slayer made a trail of arrowheads for him. The series of points went from Dennehotso through Kayenta and on top of Black Mesa. Today they call these arrowheads Comb Ridge and El Capitan. Some are black lava. Luckily, this monster ran into these arrowheads which chipped away his body, killing him. Monster Slayer collected the broken rocks that were his body and took them home as his trophy."

    Man-made arrowheads flaked from chert hold special ceremonial powers to cure and protect. Just as snakes are related to Big Snake, so, too are arrowheads connected to the world of the sacred. Monster Slayer gathered flint and learned arrowhead's protective prayers, whose power is invoked by medicine men on behalf of a patient. Flint's hardness, the sound as it rattles, and reflected light representing lightning, give it power. Horned toads use it as protection against lightning and are able to fashion their own points. A person finding an arrowhead says a small prayer and inhales over it four times. The finder offers words like, "From behind this arrowhead bad ailments will not go" or "In the four directions black arrowhead will protect me." This keeps harm away. The recipient feels, "This is a very sacred, holy thing that came into my possession." One man explained the thinking behind these protective powers. In his view, Ancestral Puebloans made these points. "The Navajo collect these arrowheads, which have already killed off enemies or dangerous animals. So the people think that because they have already killed these things, that power will ward off disease. They use them to shield the patient and others involved in a ceremony. When this protection is used, the unseen evil force goes back to where it came from."

    Another man summarized just how important arrowheads are in healing and protecting. When talking about Ancestral Puebloans and the things they left behind, he was not overly concerned, until he considered chipped points. "The arrowheads are ours. In ceremonies we hold them against our joints or put them with herbs and water to drink. They are sacred to us. . . . Lightning has an arrowhead. We are built as an arrow—our body is the stick part and our head an arrowhead. . . . May I walk in harmony, being shielded by my arrowhead. May I live a few more days."

    3. <u>Wind</u>: Just as arrowheads protect, so too, can Wind. As one of the four guards stationed outside Sun Bearer's home, Wind can take many different forms and hold various powers. Anthropologist Gladys Reichard provides an extensive list of its functions. Wind gives life—the whorls on a person's toes, fingers, and top of the head are proof that it is a life-giving force within the body; it is personified as a holy being and as a group of holy beings who assist but do not require an offering

from man; Wind mentors and can forewarn of approaching danger; it also reports events and thoughts, be they good or bad; and Wind has both a helpful and destructive side. The interconnectedness of Wind with life begins with birth and ends with death. When a child is born the winds argue as to which one is entering the body; once it does, this determines how long a person will live. "The wind will already set a day that it will leave your body and a person does not live any longer than that."

There are two different types of wind. The first is níyol or the wind that is felt blowing against the skin. This is a physical manifestation of the second type, Niłch'i, which is the spiritual force or being behind níyol and which acts in much the same way as the Christian deity, the Holy Ghost. Both are powers designed to aid, instruct, and warn. It is also something that man can appeal to and through. James McNeley's extensive study, *Holy Wind in Navajo Philosophy*, examines many of Niłch'i's functions. In relation to Comb Ridge, it is important to understand that there is a large body of teachings concerning Holy Wind, and that only part of it is discussed here.

The alcoves and potholes found along Comb Ridge are Wind's home and when the wind blows, it is moving inside. The round holes on top of the ridge are called "[Wind's] Tracks on It" and the alcoves on the side are "Tracks along Side of It." One medicine man tells of hearing the winds blow within the ridge since they are present

Photo by Kay Shumway

throughout. Anywhere along this one hundred mile stretch of rock, a person appeals to Holy Wind's power. Offerings and prayers are given to prevent Wind's harm. One time a group of people from Kayenta and Black Mesa feared the onslaught of a destructive gale. This medicine man went to the head of Comb Ridge near Tonalea. There, he placed his offering of ntł'iz, uttered a prayer, and the clouds, wind, and storm dissipated. The Twins were the ones who accepted the offering of "sacred stones" and calmed the elements. His prayer asked his "big brother [Monster Slayer] to have mercy on the people, to not come this way again," and to recognize "I am here below among these people."

  During this ceremony he "prayed from 'head to toe,' because it is said that it (Comb Ridge) is full of holy wind spirits of all kinds. . . . These days nobody does the sacred offerings. Back in our ancestors' day, one would ride, ride, and ride their horse to Comb Ridge, just to say their prayers and place their sacred offerings."

  Lack of respect can result in death. One man told a short story of how fourteen Ancestral Puebloans ascended Comb Ridge with an object that allowed them to bore holes in its alcoves and the surrounding mesas. The tool went against "nature," the winds became angered and "sucked out all the living Anasazi from their dwellings and killed them. But the Diné were put inside the mountains—way, way, way inside the mountains and were not brought out until the destruction was over."

The destructive power of wind has been a force to be reckoned with since the creation of the earth. In the beginning, First Man formed four different types of wind—White (east), Blue (south), Yellow (west), and Black (north) then placed them in his garment to make them holy. He next stationed four young men, each one in a cardinal direction, to watch over these winds and then created Striped Winds to the east and west and Twisted Winds to the south and north. "And they all are things to be feared." Big Wind is the tornado and comes in the four colors. This wind can be a messenger of future bad news and may pick up belongings. The small whirlwind that circles about an open fireplace is called the Gossiping Whirlwind. It collects bad conversation from the earth and brings it back to the Holy Beings. These and other types are holy wind people.

Wind has homes in other places. At Navajo Mountain there lies a barren spot where all of the sand has blown away. Thunderous noises come from this area called "Where the Wind Blows It Out" (Hahwiiyoołii). Two days before violent weather sets in, Wind warns, through sound, what is to happen. On the south side of Navajo Mountain on the old trail to Rainbow Bridge, there lies a large hole that descends into a rock. A whirlwind attacks those who get too close. One man threw a rock down the hole to test for depth. Finally it hit the bottom, but immediately there arose a powerful funnel of air that came out of the hole and scared the Navajo away. It is forbidden to go near these kinds of places unless the site is approached after using Wind's sacred name. On the north side of the mountain there is another large hole that is also the home of Wind.

The Comb Ridge area is a place filled with power. Different aspects of Big Snake and snakes, lightning and thunder, arrowheads and flint, winds and Níłch'i have been discussed thus far. The relationships amongst these different elements are apparent, yet to truly see their integration and how this plays across the land, one needs to return to the myths. A brief paragraph from the Wind Chant illustrates how all of them tie together and are manifest through ceremonial objects and religious sites. Briefly, a hunter near Cabezon Peak, New

Mexico, killed a deer, ate some of its intestines, turned into a blue racer snake then crawled into the cave of Big Snake. His family became concerned and searched for him. Big Fly, a mentor, sent the father to the curly-headed Wind People who instructed him about how to redeem his son through ceremonial means. The family gathered all that was needed and met the Wind People at the mouth of Big Snake's cave where they could hear him moving about. The Winds made four hoops and set them nearby. We learn: "The Wind People and Thunder People were all dressed in flint armor and they prepared offerings to the Great Snake, and the boy's father was told to present these to the Snake, and that even if he was frightened, he must not run away. So he approached, lightning flashed, but he put down the offering in spite of his fear, and as he did so, a quantity of fighting snakes approached him, among them the blue snake which he knew was his son. The father caught the blue snake and threw him outside the cave to the Wind people and they passed him through the hoops, one after the other, and as he passed through them the snake skin split off his head, body, and limbs and he finally emerged in human form again and the people rolled the hoops toward the east." These same symbols and powers are a part of the Comb Ridge landscape and imbue it with potency.

4. <u>Witchcraft</u>: Witchcraft is a malignant power feared by the Navajo, and not surprisingly, Comb Ridge is connected to it. This force is not usually discussed by the people, even medicine men, since to know too much is to indicate the possibility of practicing it. Indeed, medicine men and those who are wealthy are often accused of using this power for their own aggrandizement. Admission of practicing it leads to being outcast and the power being turned against

the person using it. There are extensive studies on this topic explaining the various forms witchcraft can take. Only a brief glimpse is given here.

Wherever there is power for good, there is also the potential for evil. The previous example comparing it to electricity which is both helpful and harmful underscores the importance of who and why it is being used. Snakes, wind, arrowheads, dinosaur tracks, water, bears, and a multitude of plants, animals, places, and objects have power for good and bad depending on the desired outcome. One medicine man told of how he went to the head of Comb Ridge near Kayenta to perform a protective ceremony. In that same area, people say that witchcraft is powerful. Caves or cracks in the rocks may be entrances that open into a witchcraft house and meeting place. Incest, the murder of close relatives, the making of corpse poison, and witches' Sabbaths occur in these rooms which are inaccessible to normal humans. Skinwalkers, or people who control supernatural evil, are said to travel a route near Sand Island Bridge very close to Comb Ridge. The trail passes by the white-tipped bluffs to the south on the way to a place where the San Juan River joins a side canyon stream. Not far from there is a home for the practitioners of evil.

5. <u>Boundaries</u>: Boundaries separate sacred from profane space. The land bounded on the south by the San Juan River, the north by Elk Ridge and the Bears Ears, the west by Navajo Blanket and Lime Ridge, and the east by Bluff, holds tremendous meaning for the Navajo people. Snakes, lightning, arrowheads, wind, bears, witchcraft, and the river are not unconnected physical entities, but powerful religious and philosophical things that lead directly to sacred teachings. Power, prayers, and protection are their theme.

Do the Navajo, then, look at Comb Ridge and its environs as a physical barrier that is a spiritual boundary of power? Definitely. One woman recalls, "Comb Ridge became a shield and boundary at the time the monsters were killed. The rocks were red and made into a ridge. It starts close from the Bears Ears. My maternal grandmother said a long time ago the boundary was made here." When asked why there was a need for a boundary, she explained that after the monsters were killed, the People still feared they might be harmed. The Holy Beings created the boundaries to be shields through ceremonies. These shielding powers "will probably be used in the future. These are very powerful and when a person makes a prayer offering there, it will serve as a shield." No single power dominates. They are all connected, each stemming from a different ceremonial belief and practice.

One man referred to Butler Wash on the east side of Comb Ridge or the side where the Utes and white men live as "outside" and Comb Wash as "inside." When Navajo people crossed the ridge heading toward Bluff, they left prayers and pollen at its height before descending. Travel is an important aspect of Navajo life, both yesterday and today. Crossing from a safe haven to a place of potential danger requires spiritual precautions and supernatural help. In the story of the Twins journeying to see their Father, a motif of travel, danger, and protection appears, a motif and concern that continues to this day for Navajo people. Another man, in recounting this tale, included many of the forces connected to Comb Ridge. "The Twins came to two large bears guarding the entrance to the Sun's home. They laid crisscross at the door. Again the boys used the sacred feather [with supernatural powers] to cross over these dangerous animals. On they went and came upon two huge snakes and they used the sacred feather to cross over the top of them and went on. Next they came to two thunder-beings who lay crisscross guarding the entrance. The boys spoke to the two thunders and used the feather to cross over them, too. Then they came to two lightning-beings that killed by flashing back and forth. They also guarded the entranceway. Once again, the boys spoke to the lightning and used the sacred feather to cross over them. Next they came upon two wind beings. It was Black Wind and Blue Wind. They lay crisscross guarding the entrance. Once more the boys crossed over. When they arrived at the door of the Sun, they encountered another guard. It was black flint. It made a "swooshing" sound as it mashed together like a pair of scissors. Once again, the boys used the sacred feather to cross over the flint stones. The two boys then reached their destination."

These same types of creatures guard part of the northern boundary of Navajo land. Undoubtedly, there are other areas surrounding the reservation that have their own protective sites and powers. For the Utah Navajo, Comb Ridge is a special place of power for protection through prayer. "You make sacred offerings here [Comb Ridge] when you are in need of special blessings. It has the 'forces' of the earth, the universe, the mountains, waters, rocks, mesas, and all the land that exists to the ends of the earth. We pray for peace, hózhǫ́ǫgo (beauty and harmony), for all living things on this earth and the universe. We pray for the environment. We pray for our protection and to live without harmful obstacles getting in our way. These were the sacred prayers of our forefathers and we still pray the same."

Photo by Kay Shumway

STOP 6
COMB WASH

N37 16.422 W109 40.669

Stop Six: Comb Wash: Comb Wash on the west side of the ridge runs parallel to Butler Wash on the east side. During the spring, water from snow melt runs down its length emptying into the San Juan River, but most of the year it is dry with the exception of a few small springs. One of these water sources was historically called Navajo Spring but to the Navajo it was "Sweet Water Coming Out" (Tółikaní Halíinii) while the narrow trail that descended Comb Ridge by it was "Trail Coming Down" (Adah Adeetiin). Close to the spring was the camp of Jim Joe, a leader in the Navajo community in this area and long-time friend of the Mormons who settled in Bluff in 1880. In the mid-1950s, blasting associated with widening the road sent large boulders tumbling below, covering the spring and a number of historic sites.

1. All of Comb Wash is called Mountain Sheep's Testicles (Naagháshí Bicho'). Some time before the Navajos went to Fort Sumner during the Long Walk period of the 1860s, a hunting party camped at the mouth of Arch Canyon above Highway 95, approximately twenty miles to the north. Two

hunters, One Who Is Reddish (Dinilchíí) and Tangle People Clan (Ta'neeszahnii), bickered over the testicles of two mountain sheep killed nearby. A wrestling match broke out over who should keep the prize, each hunter demanding that the "mountain sheep organs are mine." Other men separated the scrappers and cautioned them to settle down. Someone tossed the testicles in the fire, causing them to explode because of the moisture within, ending the dispute. The hunters packed their meat and went home. Some Navajos claim that a white rock near the campsite also looks like a sheep's organ. The wash, a trail over Comb Ridge, and one of the canyons that meet at the site also share this name. Although there is some dispute over certain geographical sites and even if "Naagháshí" is a Navajo word, knowledgeable elders in the Navajo community insist that this is the correct term and interpretation.

2. Another teaching about this wash is that during the time of the emergence from the world beneath this one, the land was wet with mud left after the waters drained to the four directions. At this time there were giant birds that flew along Comb Ridge, beating the formation and drying the wash and surrounding land with the flapping of their wings. The serrated edge of the ridge testifies of the imprints of their feathers as they flew by.

3. A story about Comb Wash links it to a very important group of ceremonies in the Evil Way (Hóchxǫ'íjí) tradition, which will be discussed later as it relates to the teachings of Changing Bear Maiden (See Stop Eighteen: The Bears Ears).

STOP 7
LIME RIDGE SNAKES

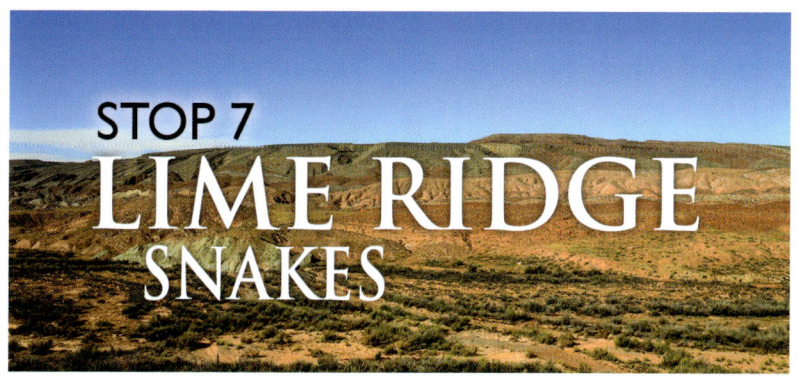

N37 15.975 W109 40.458

Stop Seven: Lime Ridge Snakes: As already mentioned, Big Snake and snakes are powerful beings that can help and protect but also harm if not shown proper respect. As you drive through Comb Ridge and look across the wash to the east side of Lime Ridge, you will see wavy lines of variegated colored sands and sandstone. The red, gray, and tan colors make a distinctive set of patterns that are snakes. On the west side of Lime Ridge is a corresponding pattern that shimmers and wriggles in the changing light—the earlier and later parts of the day making them more distinct. These are horned snakes, the one on the eastern side is male, on the western side female, and together they form a pair of protectors for this part of the reservation. When added to other snake imagery in this area, these symbols become a potent force.

    The teachings about snakes continue down the road at Navajo Blanket, which will be discussed later. The two formations are connected. One man who lived near the western base of Lime Ridge shares his experience. Speaking of the Lime Ridge formation he said, "There were snakes in that mountain at one time, but they have moved away. Where they went I do not know. Many years ago, I remember there were snakes in there. I have heard them. We used to live right around the point and could hear noises in the early dawn or at midnight, but now that has stopped. Even though they have vanished, it is still considered holy and sacred. Whenever there is an outbreak of sickness like influenza, the Diné will make offerings to it with sacred songs and prayers. It heals colds, especially the types that are fatal. Even when we were at war with foreign enemies, the Diné made sacred offerings to it. Many of our medicine men used it for protection against our enemies—the Germans and Japanese. That is where the Diné language for protection came from—the sacred language that the code talkers used against the enemy. The prayers and sacred offerings were given to the mountain because that is where all the sacred 'shake offs' [materials gathered from animals and objects with sacred protective power]—lightning, bear, Holy Wind—were derived. That is about all I can say—it's all very sacred."

    Each place discussed so far has an inner form, a spiritual essence in human form that communes with the person praying. Pollen and sacred stones, or nt'łiz, are accepted by this being. In time of war combatants or their relatives go to these places to say prayers for safety. The first time this was done, prior to the Long Walk (1860s), a group of medicine men came to the Comb Ridge—Lime Ridge—Navajo Blanket area located farther down the road (See Stop: Twelve Navajo Blanket), to create a supernatural, spiritual shield based in the power of Big Snake to protect the People. And that is why one elder asserted that through prayers offered at Navajo Blanket, "beauty will come [his] way."

STOP 8
LIME RIDGE, CREEK, & SUGAR LOAF

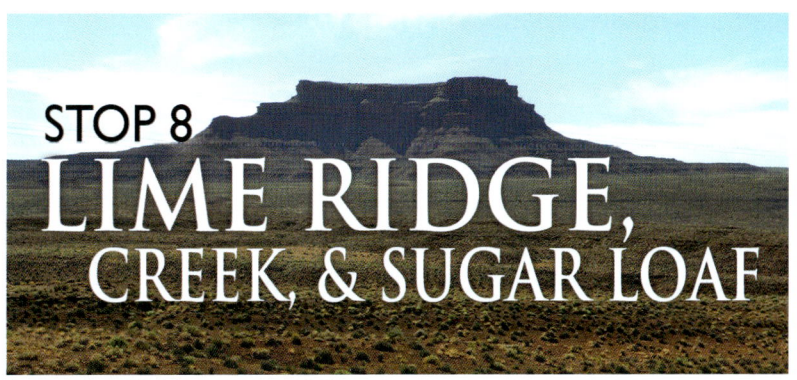

Sugar Loaf: N37 14.423 W109 47.377

Stop Eight: Lime Ridge, Lime Creek, and Sugar Loaf: Lime Ridge is composed of a base of limestone that has been pushed upward with much of its covering eroded away so that pockets of limestone are exposed on its surface. Deposits of lime extend from Comb Ridge to Cedar Mesa and have been used by local inhabitants for thousands of years. The earliest known Clovis Paleo-Indian site in San Juan County is found on Lime Ridge and has been dated to about 9,000 B.C. Archaeologists conjecture that Clovis hunters and gatherers selected this site because of its broad view of the San Juan River and Comb Wash drainages where mastodons could feed in the lushly vegetated river bottoms during the cooler and moister Ice Age period.

A later group of Native Americans, the Anasazi, also used Lime Ridge to their advantage. These Ancestral Puebloans are classified by time periods, the earliest clearly identifiable one being Basketmaker II (100 B.C.- 600 A.D.), following a transition period from Archaic to Anasazi. Archaeologists find piles of used limestone in Basketmaker II cooking areas. It is believed that the Anasazi used this rock when boiling food such as corn to help break down the amino acids present in the vegetable as well as add another amino acid, lysine, to make the diet more complete. Later, when beans rich in lysine became part of the diet, limestone was no longer necessary. Thus, piles of these rocks have become a diagnostic factor in determining the occupation of a Basketmaker II site.

Settlers in Bluff also used lime, but this time to make mortar for construction with adobe bricks. At least one pioneer kiln has been found near Lime Ridge in Butler Wash, its exterior shaped by rocks in the form of a beehive. A fire inside the kiln heated pieces of limestone until they became brittle. The worker then removed the heated rocks, crushed them when cooled, then slaked the powder with water to the consistency desired for mortar. Perhaps the person who named Lime Ridge was one of the men who worked its deposits, although Lime Creek at its western base was initially (1881) called Epsom Creek because its water was so alkaline.

To the Navajo, there are teachings that go far beyond the physical uses of this hill with its associated sites.

1. Atop Lime Ridge sits a trapezoidal block of sandstone called Sugarloaf that looks like a male or forked stick hogan as opposed to the rounded female hogan more common on the reservation today. The names have nothing to do with who uses either one—men and women have access to both. The more pointed one, which represents the earlier form of the two types—is smaller but considered more powerful—a good place to hold ceremonies. In this male hogan on Lime Ridge are trapped children who were disobedient to Jóhonaa'éí (Sun Bearer). They are being punished for their not following his divine counsel. A story tells of how the god warned them not to steal animals and to be respectful of people's property, but they repeatedly failed to do his bidding. Jóhonaa'éí placed them in the hogan for four days, trying to bring them to repentance, but when this failed, the hogan turned to solid rock. Thus important Navajo teachings of behavior—do what the Holy People say, respect property rights, be humble enough to learn—are encapsulated in this formation—now set in stone. When a person is near this site, he or she can still hear the children crying.

2. On the surface of Lime Ridge lies chert (often mistakenly called flint) scattered about, said to be the scales

or skin of Big Snake. Some people suggest that the Sugarloaf rock formation is the forehead of Big Snake, his home, or a shield that protects him. Most agree that "this ridge, where all the snakes once lived, is our shield against all bad and evil things. We bring our offerings in prayers and songs to this ridge when we need to. For example, a man and his son from Navajo Mountain asked a local medicine man for a blessing of protection. The son later left for the war in Iraq. Eventually the father returned to the medicine man and told him how his son wanted to thank him for the prayers that saved his life.

This illustrates how sacred and holy this ridge is to the Navajo and how its power reaches far beyond local realms.

3. During the time of creation, when water covered the land, it is said that the waters almost went to the top of Lime Ridge. But when the water began to drain, it went out via the San Juan River, leaving canyons on the side of the ridge made by the rivulets.

Photo by Kay Shumway

STOP 9
VALLEY OF THE GODS

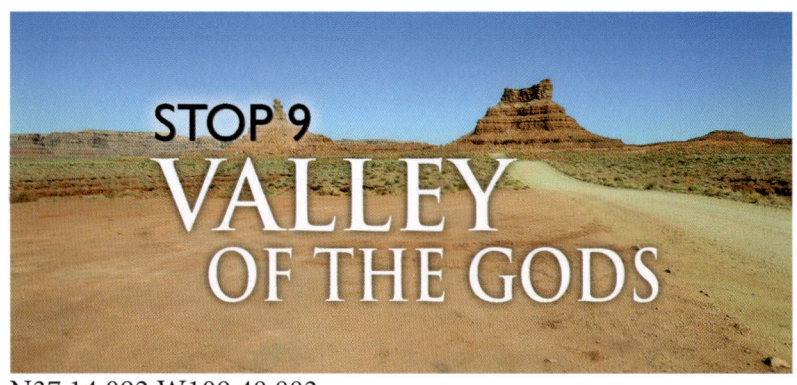

N37 14.092 W109 48.882

Stop Nine: Valley of the Gods: This dramatic landscape provides excellent examples of differential erosion in the Halgaito Shale formation. The various shapes are said to be different objects. For instance as one descends the western slope of Lime Ridge and looks to the west and north into this area, one can see a rock formation that looks like a saddle.

There are others said to be Navajo warriors frozen in stone who can be appealed to for protection. They are guardians whose power and strength aid young men going to war. By placing sacred stones (ntl'iz) at the base of one of these pinnacles, the person pleases the spirit inside, who will then provide supernatural assistance to the one whose name is mentioned or whose voice is heard in prayer. People are cautioned not to climb on these rocks for fear of offending the holy being and because one does not know to which clan or tribe these frozen warriors belong. Another prayer site for servicemen is located at the top of Long Mountain in the Shonto area. This is important to the people in the Tuba City, Navajo Mountain, Shonto, and Oljato areas.

VISITOR NOTE: *The drive through this beautiful valley is one of the favorite excursions for visitors in the area. You can access the loop via US 261 to US 163 or vise versa. The dirt road stretch is 16 miles long. High clearance vehicles recommended, but most cars can make it if weather permits and you drive with care. Jeeps can be rented in Bluff, UT.*

Photo by Kay Shumway

Photos by Kay Shumway

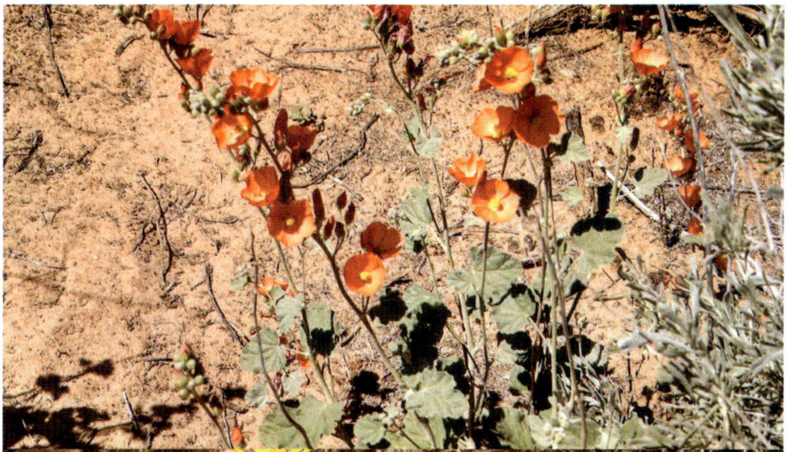

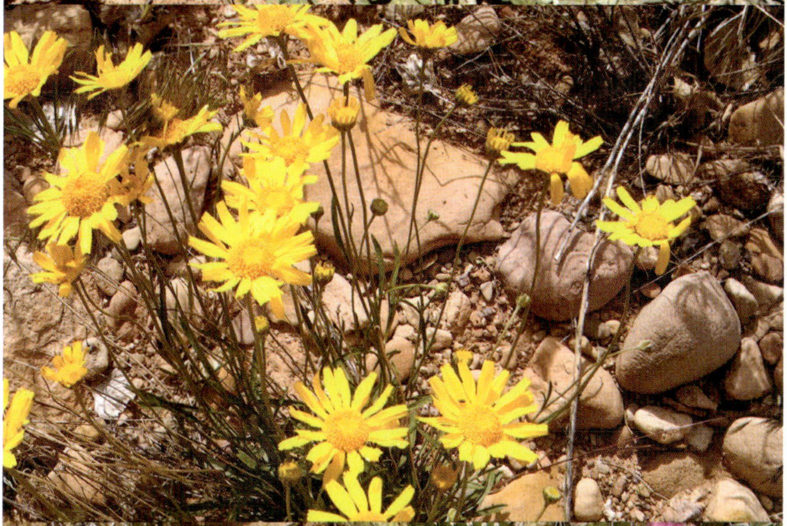

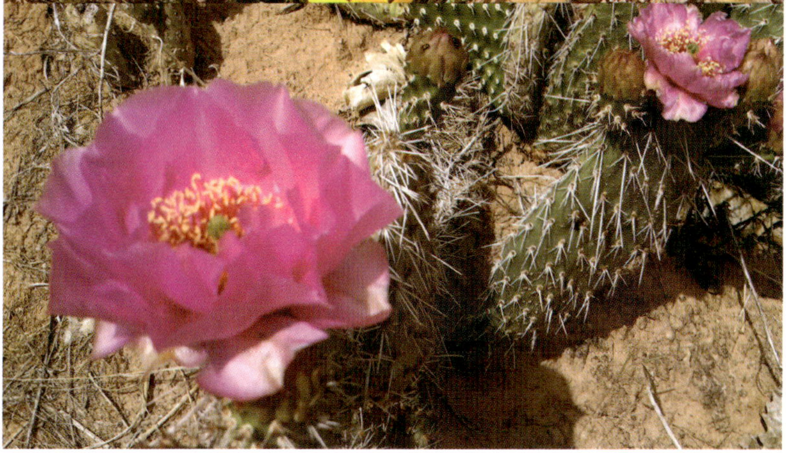

48

STOP 10
MISSING SANDSTONE BLOCK

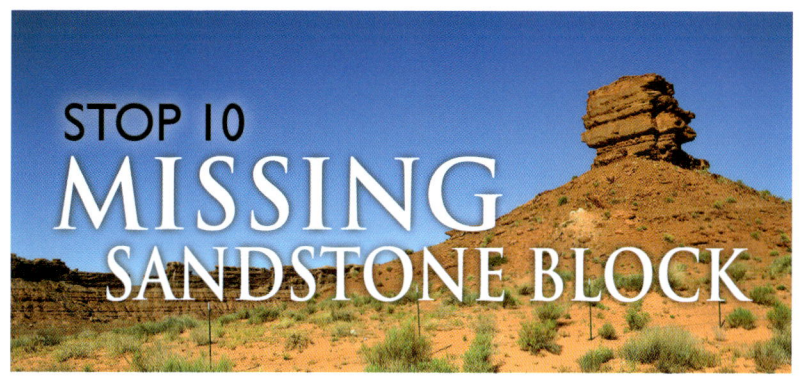

N37 13.438 W109 49.313

Stop Ten: Missing Sandstone Block: As you leave the Valley of the Gods and continue on Highway 163, there is to the left on the rock ridge paralleling the road a distinctive square of rock missing from the ledge. Next to the road, several hundred yards away, sits a conical base of stone upon which the missing square rock is said to sit. There are two stories about how the rock from the ledge was displaced.

1. One story tells of how Coyote, the trickster, who played an important role in affecting physical things in today's world, was walking along contemplating all of the troubles he had. He scuffed his foot in disgust, knocking the rock out of the ledge and onto the mound to the east where it rests today.

2. Another, more serious story returns to the time of creation, when monsters roamed the land. Some of these dangerous creatures were the One-Who- Kills-with-Its Eyes, Walking Rock, Tracking Bear, and The-One-Who- Kicks-People-Off-the-Cliff. Monster Slayer, in preparation for ridding the world of these creatures, fixed certain places for target practice. This particular spot he used to brace his weapons so that he could shoot straight. When he was pursuing a giant snake, he pushed the square rock out of its place so that he would have a clear shot. He succeeded in killing this and most of the other monsters so that the Diné could multiply across the face of the land.

STOP 11
WATER FROM THE PIPE

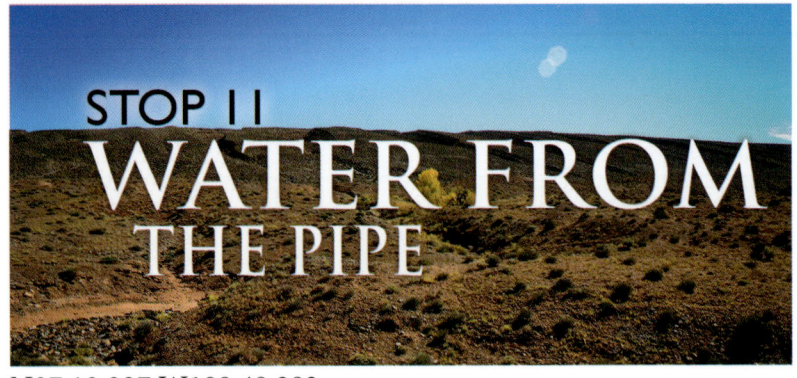

N37 13.327 W109 49.382

Stop Eleven: "Water from the Pipe": Water in a high desert climate draws people to it as iron filings to a magnet. Directly across from the missing sandstone block stands a group of trees on the side of the hill before starting up to the western snake ridge. Next to the trees and surrounded with grass is a small pool known in Navajo today as Water from the Pipe Spring (Bééshbitoo' Háálíní). While the pipe is a more modern addition, this site was a favorite meeting place for Navajo hunters heading for higher ground in search of deer in the more thickly vegetated area. One man described this practice:

"The hunters used to gather right up there, where the willows are at Water from the Pipe. They would camp out along here (beside where the road is today) too under the cottonwood trees. The horses, donkeys, and mules would be hobbled and grazed close by. There was a lot of water coming from the pipe back then."

50

STOP 12
SOUTHERN TIP OF CEDAR MESA

N37 12.023 W109 53.293

Stop Twelve: Southern Tip of Cedar Mesa: Also widely known as "Muley Point" by modern visitors, this is a favorite vista for all who venture to the top. If you turn north on HWY 261you will be approaching a massive cliff wall. With the Goosenecks State Park to your left and Valley of the Gods on your right, you are looking directly at the southern tip of Cedar Mesa. This large geographical area, first named by Mormon pioneers on their way to settle Bluff in 1880, extends from Red House Cliffs in the west, Highway 95 to the north, Comb Wash to the east, and the San Juan River to the south. Although not visible until directly upon it, there is a road called the Moki Dugway that ascends to the top of the mesa. Constructed in 1954, this series of switchbacks allowed uranium trucks to move ore from the Red Canyon—White Canyon region in the northwest to the processing mill outside of Mexican Hat.

The visible end of Cedar Mesa is called "Hanging Meat" (Atsį' dahidédlo') a name bestowed by an event that took place on top and the far side of the mesa where there is a spring called "Sagebrush Spring" (Ts'ah bito'). Part of this mesa, that projects into the eastern end of Valley of the Gods, is called Edge-of-Ridge-up-a-Rocky-slope (Adáá' tsé niinahgi), a place where hunters chased and cornered deer on the edge of the ridge. The animals could not escape and so were easily shot. The entire mesa received its name of Hanging Meat because one band of hunters was so successful that they left earlier than expected. One of the men had hung his deer meat out to dry on the branches of trees and bushes. When the hunting party departed, he went with them, never returning for the game he had left to dry. Cedar Mesa received its Navajo name from this incident.

Photo by Kay Shumway

STOP 13
GOOSENECKS

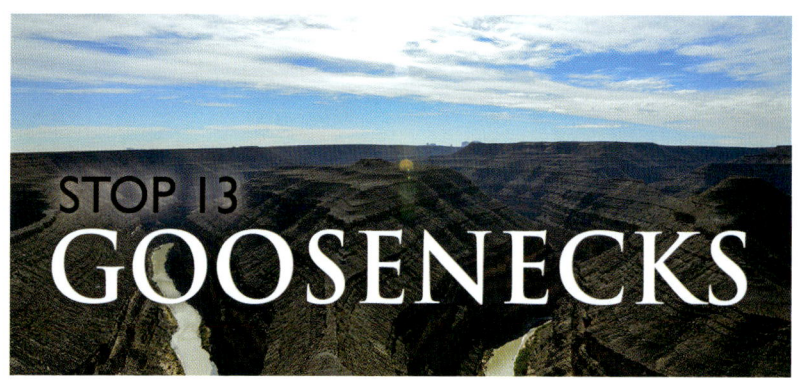

N37 10.456 W109 55.636

Stop Thirteen: The Goosenecks: The Goosenecks is a deeply entrenched meander cut by the San Juan River 1,000 feet below. This dramatic landscape has made its way into many a geography book to illustrate stream erosion whose qualities were dramatic enough to turn the area into a state park in 1962. To the Navajo, it has traditionally been a place of power and is connected to the teachings of Navajo Blanket, discussed next. The San Juan River is sometimes described as a large serpent, whose body is coiled at the Goosenecks which in Navajo is called Its Body is Crooked (Bits'íís nooltł'izihí). One person suggested that Big Snake received his nourishment by luring prey with a type of magnetic force from the Bear Ears, linking two of the most powerful and dangerous animals in Navajo religion, the Bear and Big Snake, in geographical landforms. Medicine men pray at this spot insisting that beauty in the form of protection comes because they recognize its power. In the olden days, these men fashioned objects from carnotite for protection and placed them nearby.

STOP 14
NAVAJO BLANKET

N37 11.701 W109 51.939

Stop Fourteen: Navajo Blanket: Raplee Ridge, known locally as Navajo Blanket because of its variegated sand and rock designs, is a dramatic anticline that during the early morning and late afternoon casts deepened shadows on the red, gray, and brown of the formation. The ridge's official name came from Adelbert (Dell) L. Raplee who staked mining claims for gold and oil in this area. Known to the Navajos as "Hastiin God Damn," Dell Raplee was one of a number of influential people to enter the area seeking mineral wealth and eventually establishing the town of Goodridge (later Mexican Hat).

At one point following the turn of the twentieth century, this village had a platted town site; a telephone line that connected Bluff, Blanding, and Monticello to Moab and Thompson with its Western Union terminal, a water system with eight hundred feet of pressure; a hotel and restaurant; and a population estimated at 1,500. Once the boom for oil played out, this infrastructure fell into disrepair as people abandoned the area. Dell Raplee was among the entrepreneurs who benefited momentarily from this boom and bust environment.

To the Navajo, the anticline is known as "Mountain that is Coiled" (Dził Na'neests'ee'ii), and is believed to hold two different powers.

1. The first is said to be the home of the Wind. To one person, it has been "set aside" for this purpose and should

be treated with great respect, just as it is for Big Snake, the second power. A Navajo medicine woman agrees. Speaking of Navajo Blanket, she recounts that it is the home of different winds that made the swirling marks on its exterior. There are big winds and small ones, but either one can be approached because "it is right there [Navajo Blanket] that prayers are offered." She asserts again that they live there. "Wind takes the lives of people and their homes. The big wind (tornadoes and hurricanes) are very strong. When people are disobedient, the big wind is given the right to take our lives. This is why it is greatly feared. The small ones, like a twister, are messengers. Sometimes they move clockwise and other times counter-clockwise and are like spies it is said. They also have a way of casting a spell. This type is called Young Female Twister (Ch'ikę́ę́ Naayisí) when giving it an offering. If it ever goes over you and takes a possession, you just let it go. Do not take the object back. You sprinkle the corn pollen after it and say that the thing you took from me will have no meaning now; however, if you put a spell on me the object that you took will no longer be of benefit. The curse is given when the wind takes the sweat and dirt from your body. By taking it, the wind is able to steal your thinking and you become confused. Sometime, in the days that follow, when the people go in deceitful ways where it looks like there is no more hope, Big Wind has been given the right to take up their lives, just as he did with the Anasazi. . . . If there is nothing wrong with your place, it won't come to your home or bother your livestock. Only when something is bothering your household will it do this. This is what is said."

2. As with many other formations in the area, Navajo Blanket is also associated with Big Snake. The pattern on the hill reflects the same design of the giant bull snake (díyóósh) that lives inside. People who have tried to uncoil this snake have been hissed at with large puffs of air. Bad luck accompanies those who trespass this area and do not show respect. For instance people have drowned in the river below, said to have been killed by the snake that slips down to the water. Big Snake can also wriggle over the ground without touching it and can harm a person mentally just by being present. When people disappear in this area, it is credited to the serpent; and when an oil company could not drill successfully at a site near here, it was because the snake kept pushing the drill bit out of the earth. Even white men have died here because of its power.

Photo by Kay Shumway

STOP 15
MEXICAN HAT

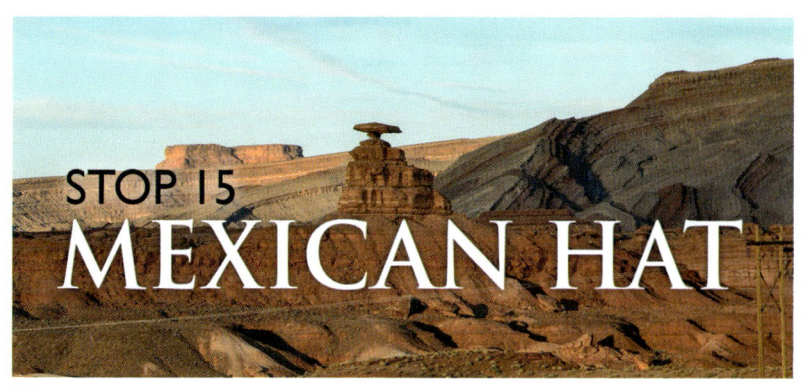

N37 10.498 W109 51.572

Stop Fifteen: Mexican Hat Rock and Spencer Trading Post: As one proceeds down the highway with the San Juan River on the left, there soon appears Mexican Hat Rock, known in Navajo as Ch'ah łizhin or Black Hat. While the formation has the shape of a sombrero on end, the name Black Hat may have come from a white man named Bill Young, whose Navajo name was Black Hat, or from another person whose identifying characteristic came from his apparel. For whatever reason, this much-photographed formation gave the nearby town its name. Close to where the main road intersects with the dirt road that goes to the rock, there used to be an old wooden trading post in operation from 1911-1931. Built by John L. Oliver (Tsiiyaa Nichxọ'ii – Dirty or Ugly Neck) in 1911, the post was soon (around 1914) leased to Arthur H. Spencer (Bilagáana Tsoh – Big Whiteman) who spent a number of years running the facility before Oliver resumed operation. Navajos and Utes were the standard customers, with merchandise on the shelves coming from as close as Bluff and as far away as southwestern Colorado (Dolores, Durango, and Mancos) as well as stores further south in New Mexico. In exchange Navajos traded sheep, blankets, and jewelry. In 1925, Ray Hunt leased the post for a few years before turning it and its inventory over to Cord Bowen and Dan Tyce. They managed the store until 1931 when it was torn down.

  In addition to the trading post proper there were also a series of tents and outbuildings that increased as the years went on. In 1920 traveler Charles H. Bernheimer described the post and his visit this way: "The trader was Mr. J. H. Oliver, a Mormon and the first 'Wilson Democrat' I met on my travels . . . cheerful, pleasing, if filthy personality. All he had was a one room shack built from the lumber of deserted gambling dens that at one time existed there twenty years ago during an oil boom. The chairs were boards nailed together, so was his table and bed. Many hundreds of empty tin cans lay around, and as far as the eye could reach there was neither tree nor bush to break the monotony of this rusty tin can trading post. . . . Supper in his shack, and I did not enjoy it . . . sand in . . . stewed prunes and bread as hard as pavorrazzo marble with blue and pink mold from age . . . can you think of this man being sued for divorce and alimony by his wife? A couple of cheap Navajo horses, a dozen head of cattle, and $1,500 worth of goods in his trading store seems all the income producing values he possesses; besides he was lame. He had a fine head on his shoulders, though . . . looked like the best looking U. S. senator and almost conversed as well, only a bit more 'roughnecky', and he could sing. And he did by moonlight after supper. . . . It would have been beautiful if it had not been so droll."

      Across the road and still visible are the remains of a "guest hogan" used by travelers who came to trade and spend the night before starting the return trip. This was a common practice for traders who did what they could to lure customers and keep them trading at their post. Visitors often received some treats and gifts in the store while the hogan might be supplied with basic necessities, firewood, and utensils to make the occupants happy. Grace Hunt was constantly after her husband who loaned her pots and pans to Indian visitors. The Navajo people were great travelers and were not tied to a particular trading post just because it was close by. A survey conducted in the early 1900s in this area indicates that people regularly traveled in a sixty mile radius for their shopping needs. Their relationship with a particular trader was a key element in their deciding to be a return customer.

A Navajo eyewitness account of this post in the 1920s describes its role in the community: "The Navajos were living around that area back then, in the red rocky hills west of Mexican Hat Rock. We used to live there, too. The store was small but nice. The people made an irrigation ditch all the way from the San Juan River by the Hat rock to the store so that they could have a supply of water. [Arthur Spencer] used to buy sheep and goats from the Navajos so he kept his store well-supplied with flour, potatoes, and other groceries. I only bought striped candy canes since I was still a little boy. People bought things over the counter while the trader stood behind the counter. The store was quite large and built with wood. There was also a guest hogan for the Navajo customers. The hogan was built halfway up with rocks, and the rest was made with logs, bark, and sand."

Original Guest Hogan

Another Navajo man shares his experience as a customer during the same period: "It was close to summer when the sheep had their lambs. My older brother had good fat lambs. His two wives and children had their sheep and my mother's sheep in the same herd. I started to herd the lambs to Mexican Hat with the understanding that my older brother would follow me a little later. There were four of them riding behind me—my brother and his two wives and Woman Who Owns the House (Adzáán Bikinii). We crossed the wash that comes from Monument Valley. They had brought my lunch, and while I was eating, the others kept on herding the sheep.

After I finished my lunch, I took after them. They had already gone quite a ways and were close to Mexican Hat. We crossed the river, where a white man named [Big Whiteman] was running the trading post, but the person who bought the sheep looked like a Mexican. I bought a pair of blue jeans but do not remember how much money I received. The trader said that the lambs were big and fat and that he had not seen lambs that big. My brother said that he bought a ram from a white man and the trader said no wonder the lambs were fine looking. Some people had come to see the sale, and one person asked my brother how he had gotten such a good price on the lambs. The trader said it was because the lambs looked very good. We settled in for the night right there, and the women started to cook.

"We had used five horses to get the lambs to Mexican Hat. I hobbled the horses at Mexican Hat rock for the night. The next morning at dawn, I brought them back. There was pressed hay provided by the trader for the horses near where we slept. He probably bought his hay from Blanding because it was hard to grow things in the Mexican Hat area."

"When we got home before sunset, we had a lot of goods. Woman Who Owns the House bought a shawl, fabric, and food, some of which my brother's children ate. When we were still in Mexican Hat, my older brother had asked me to buy some food for my mother so I purchased a fifty pound sack of flour which cost $3.50, and took it to her. I also bought her coffee and twenty-five cents worth of

Arthur Spencer at Old Mexican Hat Trading Post

sugar. She was thankful for the food and for the way I acted. Then one of my younger brothers, Little Dove, came to see her because he thought maybe she was running out of food. My mother said she had plenty of food since I had just brought some to her. My younger brother thanked me for it. At other times I would herd sheep for my mother or bring her firewood, as did my younger brother."

From these two accounts one can see how trading posts became an integral part of a far flung Navajo community dependent upon their services to meet the needs in a livestock economy. Wool, woven products, and the animals themselves were important commodities whose value fluctuated with trends in the more general American economy. A second point taken from these narratives is the cooperative family effort where sharing and service strengthened kinship ties. Navajo culture stresses the importance of matrilineal lines with the mother and grandmother exerting strong influence in the direction an entire family should go. Those with the ability and means to care for family members had the responsibility to assist those who could not. This characteristic is still important today.

Utes and Paiutes also traded at the Mexican Hat Post. As in any business, there were good and bad customers as well as prosperous and impoverished times. The year 1915 proved to be the latter. It started with a running gunfight in Bluff in which a marshal tried to arrest a Ute man accused of killing a Mexican sheepherder in Colorado. Little went well during the process which ended with people being killed on both sides before the Utes fled town. Trader Arthur Spencer found that as soon as the conflict started, the Utes lost all of their food and "would come down on me and, of course, their being broke and no other tribes to help them, they had to eat. The only thing I could do was to feed them and take a chance on getting the money out of them when they were able to pay it. In doing this they eventually left a bill of several hundred dollars which I never collected." Trader-customer relations were paramount to continued post operations.

STOP 16
SAN JUAN TRADING POST

N37 09.088 W109 52.056

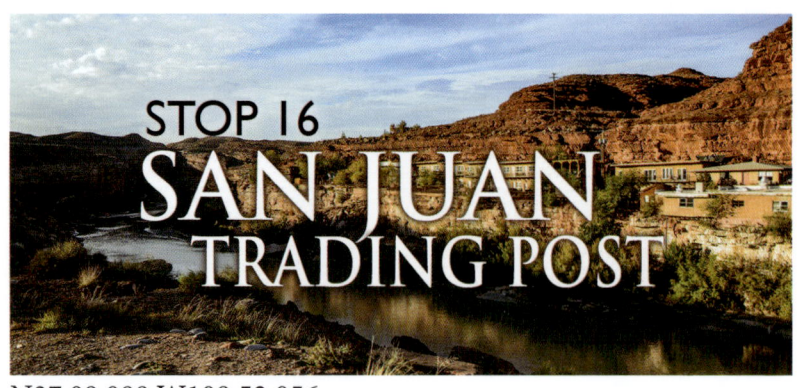

Stop Sixteen: San Juan Trading Post on San Juan River: Today as one travels through the town of Mexican Hat with stores, motels, and other buildings lining both sides of the road, it is difficult to imagine what it looked like during the gold rush and oil boom of the last decade of the nineteenth and first decade of the twentieth century. The excitement of the boom and the disappointment of the bust encouraged a fleeting dream that left its debris throughout the area. The only lasting economic institution was the trading post and so less than ten years after the one around Mexican Hat Rock closed, another started up, this time in the bend of the road next to the bridge. Actually the first trading posts no doubt were part of the town of Goodridge, later renamed Mexican Hat. Among the earliest traders to work in this area were Emery L. Goodridge, Art and Medora Spencer, Cord and Augusta Bowen, and Ray Hunt, but the actual location of the tent stores and primitive buildings are unclear. What is for certain is that in 1937, a man named Dan Tyce established the one by the river but remained in business for only a short time, because of pressure placed on him by his neighbor, Norman Nevilles, to close the post. He sold the one-building operation to Merritt Smith who sold it to June Powell all in a short period of time. In 1939, Ray Hunt with his newly-wed wife Grace returned to the area, bypassed the old Mexican Hat location, and set up a tent to live in next to the store on the San Juan River. A bridge spanned the water bringing the flow of human traffic to the post's door. Located on the edge of the reservation, Hunt began buying sheep that the Navajos were forced to relinquish because of the government-enforced livestock reduction. He grazed his growing flock of over a thousand sheep along the banks of the river and sold the animals in Colorado. He also traded with Navajo customers for wool and blankets.

The trading post, fashioned from nearby quarried stone and lumber salvaged from abandoned structures or hauled in from Bluff, protected the trade goods. Eventually the Hunts left their tent for a more permanent structure, but life was still primitive. Drinking water came from the river and was stored in four fifty gallon drums that allowed the sediment to settle over a twenty-four hour period before drinking it. Until a kerosene-powered refrigerator arrived, a wooden framed box covered with dampened burlap sacks to keep the evaporative cooling process underway, preserved fresh food. Located under the shade of the bridge, this cooler required constant attention to keep the cloth damp. Since the tent and later the store could become oppressively hot during the summer, chairs under the bridge also provided a shady living room cooled by river breezes. Clothes washing was not nearly as convenient or comfortable since the river water had to be hauled to the site, boiled over an open fire, then changed for rinsing, all of which was done in the hot sun.

Harry Goulding, Grace Hunt, Ray Hunt, Mike Goulding, Maurice Knee

By 1944, Ray and Grace Hunt were ready for a change and so leased the post to a man named John Johnson, who in 1947 turned it over to Jim Hunt, Ray's brother. Jim built living quarters over the trading post and added twenty-one motel units beside it for visiting tourists. Many of these were occupied by travelers during the river-running season when they arrived for a San Juan River boating adventure with Norman Nevilles. He was an avid boater, tour guide, and promoter of the river running experience on many rivers in southeastern Utah, two of his favorites being the San Juan and Colorado Rivers.

From a Navajo perspective, the Mexican Hat Trading post was vital for three different reasons. The first and most obvious was that it was a place to trade Navajo products for the staples of life. Rugs and wool were the mainstay but that shifted following the livestock reduction of the 1930s. Pawn or the ability to receive credit based on leaving an object of value with the trader for an extended period of time until it could be redeemed was an appealing system given the annual cycles of wealth and poverty. As dependence on livestock became less economically viable for a Navajo family in the late 1940s and 1950s, there were other means of livelihood advertised through the post. The introduction of uranium mining in the region called for skilled and unskilled laborers to apply for jobs. The same was true of the movie industry that recognized the photogenic qualities of Monument Valley and the surrounding area.

Agents for both industries used the posts as a hub for recruitment and services available in Navajo communities. The Mexican Hat Trading Post was no exception. Mail, check-cashing, and community notices were all part of this growth into the mid-twentieth century. Finally, the posts introduced social and cultural change to its customers. The Navajo people have always been selective, choosing new technology or other innovations that fit into their cultural beliefs. Unlike some tribes flooded with cultural change, the Navajo lived a more isolated life that allowed them to pick and choose at a more leisurely rate. Consequently their language and beliefs remained more intact than many other tribes. Traders were wise to what their customers wanted and provided it accordingly.

An excellent account of activities at the post during Ray Hunt's time is provided by a Navajo sheepherder named Navajo Oshley who worked for him. The experience gives a feeling for those difficult days when men, not machines, performed laborious tasks. Oshley tells of returning to

Mexican Hat: "The trader, Ray Hunt, was standing in the doorway with his brother, who was deaf. He looked tired as he walked slowly back into the trading post. He had taken the sheep—there were only a few—back to the river. Hunt was very happy to see me, saying hello, calling me his brother, and shaking my hand. I took my saddle down from my horse and set it on the sand. I got some firewood, and he brought me some water, coffee, and food. It was evening by the time I had finished eating, but he stayed late with me into the night.
"The next day, I got up and took the sheep out just as the sun rose. I let them graze and set the coffeepot on the hot coals. After I finished my coffee, I went after the sheep, which had remained nearby because they were satisfied with where they were. I tried to herd them to another place, but they would not budge. I went back to the trading post, and the trader asked me if I had eaten. I told him that I had, but he gave me some water then I took off again. When I got back to the sheep, it was hot so I thought I should take them down to the river before it got really hot. I tried to make them move a little faster, but they just took their time.

"When I got there, it was noon so the sheep went under the shaded area on the side of the rock where the hill slopes into the ground. The sheep stayed there and I went back to the trading post where I cooked my lunch and ate. Then I got worried that a coyote might go by the sheep, so I went back to where they were. I did not know that the sheep were used to roaming around by themselves, and here I was going back and forth while the sheep were staying there. I started washing my clothes and myself. When it got a little cooler, I took the sheep back to the river again.

"After they drank, I wanted to have them go back toward the trading post, but they still wanted to roam around in the canyon. When the sun was about to go down, I had finally gotten them back to the corral. Then Hunt came to me and said that they just let the sheep out and let them roam around by themselves, and that all I had to do was keep an eye on them. I said that I was afraid of what might happen to them, but he said that he didn't think that there was anything to worry about. Since my wife was still in Dennehotso drying the corn, I just slept anywhere near the trading post. I was doing this work to pay off the debt on the saddle [previously bought in Dennehotso on credit at a post] at the rate of one dollar a day. I was well taken care of and was there for many days. . . .

"One time my employer asked me if I wanted to fix a sack lunch to take with me, and I said that it was up to him. He made my lunches and I tried my best to take care of his sheep because he really took care of me. He thought I was a very good sheepherder. He never told me which way I should herd the sheep, and if I asked, he would say that I knew the best place to take them, where there were plenty of shrubs and grass. He did not care if I herded the sheep where I wanted. He told me that a man had recommended me, saying that I was a really good worker, and that was true.

"The road to Bluff City was in poor condition in those days. I do not know how many times the trader in Mexican Hat went to Bluff to get supplies in his old vehicle, but I do know that it kept stopping on him. [Ray Hunt described his vehicle as a "stripped down Ford with a box on the back." Comb Ridge was so steep and difficult to traverse that he had a bicycle pump installed in the fuel system so that as he drove, an assistant could hand-pump enough gas to the engine to propel the car up the grade.] He also had a telephone line, but it was in poor condition. [By 1910 a telephone system extended from

Monticello through Blanding and Bluff to Mexican Hat. All calls were routed by an operator in Monticello, who, through a system of long-and-short-rings, identified which phone in the system should receive the call. The line constantly needed repair, especially the section extending to Mexican Hat. Ray Hunt remembers going outside his post and pouring water on the ground wire to improve reception.]

"One evening at sunset, I had gotten the sheep in and was eating supper when the deaf white man who assisted the trader came to see me. He told me to come in and listen, then handed me the phone. My employer was making the call from Bluff and asked me to take the sheep out and head for Bluff the next morning at dawn. He said it would take me two days to get there and he agreed that I should herd the sheep slowly and not rush them. I told him that if he wasn't joking about it, it would happen. I also told him that I had very little food left, but he said that the deaf person would prepare the camping food. I gave the telephone back and went outside to sleep.

"The next morning, I took the sheep and food such as crackers, pop, and other goods, as well as my one blanket, and started to drive the sheep toward Bluff City. It was getting a little cold by this time. Across from Comb Ridge, there is a big hill [Lime Ridge], where I spent the night and kept the fire going. The following morning, I herded the sheep, then let them graze near Comb Ridge. By the time the sun was setting, I camped at Navajo Spring, where I spent the night with the sheep lying against the rock walls so they would not try to run off.

"The next morning before dawn, I built a fire and cooked the little bit of food that I had left. I got the sheep to Bluff just as the sun came up. My employer came out, told me that my debt was paid off and then got me some food. He wrote down on a piece of paper how I was to be paid and how much I had left to pay on the price of the saddle. I was very happy to go back to Dennehotso. I arrived at the trading post just before sundown. At that point in my life I was a fast traveler. The saddle was paid off, and I had a little bit of money left over."

STOP 17
ALHAMBRA AND HALCHITA

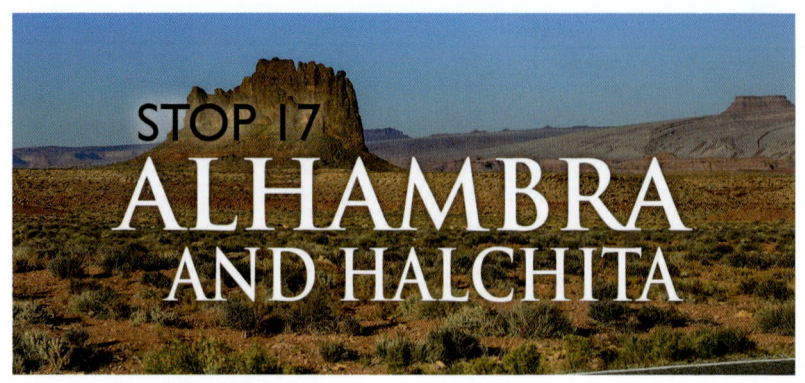

N37 07.691 W109 54.970

Stop Seventeen: Alhambra and Halchita: Traveling across the San Juan River and reaching the first flat of higher ground, you encounter two prominent features. On the west side of the road is a large volcanic neck of igneous rock named Alhambra by geologist Herbert E. Gregory in 1915. The various spires in the formation apparently reminded him of the Moorish castle in Spain of the same name. To the Navajo it is called "Black Rock Sticking from Ground (Tsé Łizhin Íí'áhá) or simply Black Rock (Tsé Łizhin) and is a sky supporter. Others say it is a group of holy people performing a Yé'ii Bicheii dance—an important ceremonial—who became frozen in stone. This ceremony is performed in late fall and during the winter to heal the sick. It is a very sacred event that lasts for nine nights and eight days and is carried out by masked and unmasked men who assume the role of deities, performing various rites and services in preparation for the final night's performance. The ceremony heals people who are losing their eyesight, hearing, or are paraplegic.

A final explanation about the powers of this rock is associated with the Evil Way (literally Ugly Way--Hóchxọ'íjí) ceremony that rids a patient of ghost sickness. The rite lasts for three or five days and removes the influence of ghosts of non-foreign enemies while another ceremony, the Enemy Way (Anaa'jí) removes ghosts that are foreign. The most prominent ceremonial characteristics include blackening (jint'eesh) the patient's body with ashes, brushing evil away from the patient with an eagle feather fan, and cutting yucca fiber tied around parts of the patient's body. All of this is accompanied by extensive songs and prayers. The blackening keeps the evil away since the patient becomes invisible to ghosts after its application. The color produced by the ashes is considered powerful because it is categorized with things that are burned by power—fire, lightning, and, in the case of a volcanic neck, geothermal heat. Alhambra sits there a product of these sacred forces, and so as with similar rock formations, should not be climbed or in any way shown disrespect. Associated with the blackening in the ceremony, Black Rock is dead, is associated with those who have passed on, and so becomes a "connecting link" where medicine men and patients go to make prayers and offerings transmitted to the realm of the dead residing in the north whose symbolic color is black. Elders from the Mexican Hat area consider this rock formation important for their well-being.

    This general area centered in the compound across the road on the east is known as Halchita (Halchíítah—In the Red Area [Land]). The small square houses visible in this valley are remnants of workers' homes who labored in a uranium processing plant in operation from 1957 to 1965. Although there were thirty-one small uranium mines in the Mexican Hat area, the vast majority of the radioactive material came from the White Canyon area transported down the Moki Dugway or from the Caine Valley region of Monument Valley. The mill was capable of processing 775 tons of ore a day. At its height, the mill complex consisted of 555 acres on which sat the mill, an acid plant, an eighty-nine unit trailer court, twenty-six miles of electrical power line, a water plant, sixty-six houses, a service station, a recreation hall, a dormitory with dining facility, a small school, a post office, the main office, a dispensary, a store, and a laboratory that served the roughly three hundred people employed there and their families. The doors of the mill closed in 1965 but the acid plant continued for another five years until the entire facility reverted to the Navajo Nation in 1970.

The large light gray area is part of the site mitigation process completed in 1995. Known as the Mexican Hat Disposal Cell, radioactive material is buried here from the mill, as well as from another facility located fifteen miles southwest, near Monument Valley, which was in operation from 1955 to 1968. From this site came 1.3 million tons of tailings hauled in by truck in the early 1990s. It was combined with demolished buildings and tailings from the Mexican Hat mill site, along with 11 buildings in the area that were constructed with contaminated tailings material, including a school, for a total of 4.4 million dry tons of material (3.1 million cubic yards). This contaminated material is covered by a twenty-four inch thick radon barrier and about 20 inches of coarsely crushed riprap rock. The disposal cell is 1,400 feet long and covers approximately sixty-eight acres. The clean-up and cell was done as part of the Department of Energy's Uranium Mill Tailings Remedial Action Project on Navajo Nation land.

A Navajo worker explains his experience at the mill. "I was hired in Mexican Hat at the uranium-processing mill to work the graveyard shift. The ore was ground to sand, sifted, and refined, then mixed with water and run through some pipes overhead. Underneath were huge pots of black tar heated by flames, which dried the ore all night long. Once it was dried, the workers loaded the ore into wheelbarrows and dumped it in a pile. The sifted, powdered product was dried separately, and then shoveled into the dump trucks by hand. The ore was as fine as flour and covered us from head to toe in powder, but we never knew how dangerous it was to our health."

STOP 18
BEARS EARS

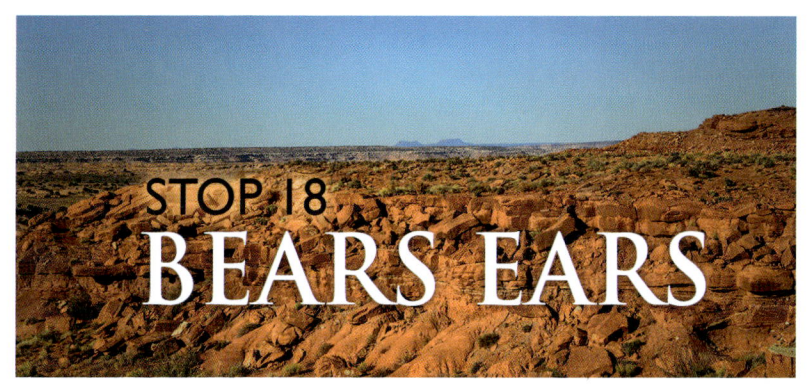

N37 16.506 W109 42.668 and N37 04.001 W110 03.779

Stop Eighteen: Bears Ears: Once you have ascended the switchbacks that leave Halchita behind for more level ground, you will see to the northwest the Bears Ears, an important site in Navajo thought. The Bears Ears aren't spectacular in themselves, the two peaks reaching only 9,059 and 8,508 feet respectively, but they are visible from long distances in the Four Corners area and have served as a regional navigation point as early as Spanish entradas into southeastern Utah. To the Spanish they were Orejas del Oso, to the Navajo Shashjaa', and the Utes Kwiyagat Nügavat, all of which translate as "Bears Ears." Geologically these two buttes are remnants of Wingate Sandstone resting on top of the Chinle formation at the end of Elk Ridge.

The Bears Ears is not only the home of bears, but is an important site in a rich body of lore. Bears' sacred names—Reared in the Mountains, Roaming in the Mountains, and Roaming in the Woods—reflect the connection to high forested areas that sit above the desert floor. Navajo mythology tells of how Bear joined Wind, Thunder, and Big Snake as one of the protectors at the entryway of Sun Bearer's home. Bear and Big Snake served as guardians of Changing Woman, Sun Bearer's wife and mother of the Twins. And when the Navajo people traveled about after their emergence, these two animals protected them from enemies.

The Female Mountain Way tells the story of two sisters who visited various locations in their quest to become reunited.

One woman wandered to the Bears Ears and spent the night. There she met some bears, played with them, and then sat upon a bluff and sang a song of loneliness. The next day she moved on, but her example is still followed today. Bears figure prominently in the ceremony derived from this story. It explains why bears of all kinds are associated with mountains and what to do when a person suffers from loneliness, sadness, or excessive weight loss. A medicine man may bring his patient to the Bears Ears, where the two may sing songs of comfort. Before and after a Blessing Way ceremony, people may go there for a short prayer and to dispose of yucca suds and materials from the sand paintings used to heal them.

The Bears Ears is also a male guardian, one of a pair, that protects Big Sheep Mountain (Dibé Ntsaa—Mount Hesperus, Colorado, mountain of the North) one of the four sacred mountains. The female counterpart to the Bears Ears is in the Carrizo Mountains (Dziłná'oodiłii—literally: The Rope-like Thing Going Around the Mountain—referring to a rainbow the people followed during the clan migrations). It is said they talk to each other, one facing out, the other in. Discussion of this Bear is found in the story of the Twins, who killed various monsters to make the earth safe for mankind. Tracking Bear, one of these evil beings, lived in the Carrizos and was destroyed. Bears as paired guardians are a common motif in the sand paintings of the Mountain Way, where they protect an entrance from evil. One woman explains: "When the two bears are brought together, they take care of the mountain. For this reason, they have the shashchíín—miniature bears made out of special stones such as turquoise and jet--which are used when prayers are offered. The ones who have these are the ones who hold special prayers to ward off evil. . . . It is like this within the Navajo boundaries. The bear is standing to guard and another bear is guarding the opposite side. For that reason, when a prayer is offered, there is a part that says the Great Dark Black Bear will stand guard, you will walk to protect or shield me." A different-colored bear may be called from each of the directions, bringing with it flint points to keep harm from the patient.

Bears not only protect but also harm people and are connected to evil, sickness, and death. The roots of the Evil Way ceremony (Hóchxǫ'íjí) lie in the lengthy narrative of Changing Bear Maiden. Despite small variations in the story that arise from the oral tradition, its main events tell of a young virtuous woman who lives with her brothers. Changing Bear Maiden is often associated with evil and mental illness. For instance, "when a person loses his mind or becomes insane . . . [or starts] to rattle their teeth or gnash them," a figurine of her as well as prayer sticks, are carved and placed with offerings at a sacred site. An individual may have nose bleeds, crazy thoughts, and dreams about mountains that enter their mind. The Evil Way ceremony stops this.

The story of Changing Bear Maiden starts with a beautiful young woman who refused wedlock to many suitors. She lived with her twelve brothers, kept a neat home, and had a decorous life. One day, coyote wandered into camp and asked her to marry him, but she gave him a series of challenges to overcome before she would accept. Through trickery and magic, he completed his tests, though both the girl and her brothers wished that he had failed. The woman kept her word, however, married Coyote, and started to learn his devious ways and evil knowledge. The brothers took him hunting but felt no love for their in-law, who wandered off to a series of adventures and mishaps. The woman, however, had been contaminated. She assumed the qualities of evil, disorder, and the ability to change into a bear—hence her name, Changing Bear Maiden.

Her brothers became increasingly concerned about the strange behavior of their sister, and so they sent the youngest brother to spy on her. He watched as she secretly assumed the qualities of a bear through ritual behavior. She faced the four directions, pulled out her eyeteeth and inserted bone awls in their stead. Hair spread over her body, her ears wagged, her snout grew longer, her nails turned to claws, and her teeth made a fearful gnashing noise. The youngest brother reported what he had seen to his brothers, who then chose to remain at home.

For four days the sister went in search of her missing husband, who had failed to return. Her anger was taken out on those she met. Each time she returned home with arrows stuck in her flesh from the enemies she fought, and each time she shook them out of her body. When her brothers left for the four directions to go hunting, she methodically tracked them down and killed them—all except the youngest one who was hidden in a hole in the ground covered over by rocks and dirt. The Holy Wind (Níłch'i) served as his guardian. Changing Bear Maiden returned to her camp in search of the sole survivor. She excreted on the ground, saying that whichever direction her stool fell or her urine flowed, there she would find her brother. They just stood up straight and puddled, so she dug down, found her brother, and then offered to help comb his hair and get him cleaned up.

Wind warned him to sit so that the sun would cast a shadow of his sister for him to watch. Just before she bent close to him for the fifth time, he sprang to his feet, ran to a bush where she had hidden her vital organs, and let fly a lightning arrow. Blood gushed forth from the bush as well as the bear. Wind warned that if the two separate streams of blood should meet, she would revive and be even harder to kill and so the brother took a knife and made a deep furrow to keep the liquids apart.

He next addressed the body and said, "You shall live again but no longer as the mischievous bear-woman. You shall live in other forms where you may be of service to your kind and not a thing of evil." He cut off her vagina and tossed it into a tree where it became a porcupine. He did the same with the left nipple, and it became piñon nuts; the right one became acorns, the glands within the breast yucca fruit, and her entrails sorrel, dock, and other plants. Her paunch he dragged to the water, which became alkali, her limbs became various types of bears which he sent off with a strict warning to behave. The head, which he threw away, is now the Bears Ears, while the furrow dug with his knife is Comb Ridge and Wash. By these actions good triumphed over evil and all of the slain brothers came back to life.

    This story illustrates important values in Navajo culture. The woman changed from a respected and talented girl to the height of evil, killing family members and losing control of her human faculties. Impurity, filth, and disorder became her way of life, and Coyote dominated her thoughts and actions. One of the Evil Way chants, called Upward Reaching Way, recounts this story with destruction of evil and pain as a central theme. Patients who have evil dreams recount through songs and prayers the story in order to be cured.

    Changing Bear Maiden is often responsible for mental illness. For instance, if one walks or sleeps where a bear has been, gets ants on him that have been on a bear, uses brush cut by a bear, drinks at its watering place, steps on its tracks, or talks or dreams of one, that person's hearing may be affected or he may become weak. Ceremonies are required to rectify the situation. Because of this story, plants used to cure witchcraft and incest are picked on the Bears Ears. Once gathered, they are crushed and sprinkled around the home in a clockwise manner, the person being careful never to complete the circle and trap the evil in. Since Coyote was the one who helped bring about death and destruction, when a coyote howls near a home, it could mean that death will come to the family living there.

The Bears Ears also play an important part in Navajo history. The earliest dated hogan ring north of the San Juan River is in White Canyon, west of the Bears Ears. In 1801, Kaa'yéłii (One with Arrow Quiver) an important local Navajo leader, was born on Elk Ridge and his brother, Manuelito, a prominent tribal leader, was born shortly after. During the trauma of the 1860s, Kaa'yeełii established a camp with five or six hogans near a canyon called Naznidzoodii (Place to Escape from the Enemy) that facilitated hidden movement off Elk Ridge. Today, the ranger station located near Kigalia Spring (an Anglicized name for Kaa'yéłii) is close to this early Navajo campsite, where he remained to avoid the general Navajo roundup and movement of Navajos to Fort Sumner, New Mexico.

Photo by Kay Shumway

Some Navajos suggest that the Bears Ears served as a boundary between Ute and Navajo holdings, though in reality it was more likely a general-use area established between the two in later times. The boundary passed between the ears and extended down Comb Ridge to Oljato; everything west of that line was Navajo and everything east of it belonged to the enemy. This boundary passes by the serpent guards on Lime Ridge mentioned earlier. Even in Navajo mythology the close proximity of the Utes to the Bears Ears, Allen Canyon, and Hammond Canyon is recognized. The wandering sister in search of her kin shares another view: "That point extending is called the Bears Ears. It is the Ute's mountain. Take care not to go there." And later, when two holy beings visit this place they comment, "We went around on Bears Ears to the home of the earth surface people. Their language was very abusive; earth surface people have no regard for holy things; that is evident." This probably refers to the Utes in the area, since the Navajo knew how to show proper respect.

STOP 19
WHITE TIPPED MOUNTAIN

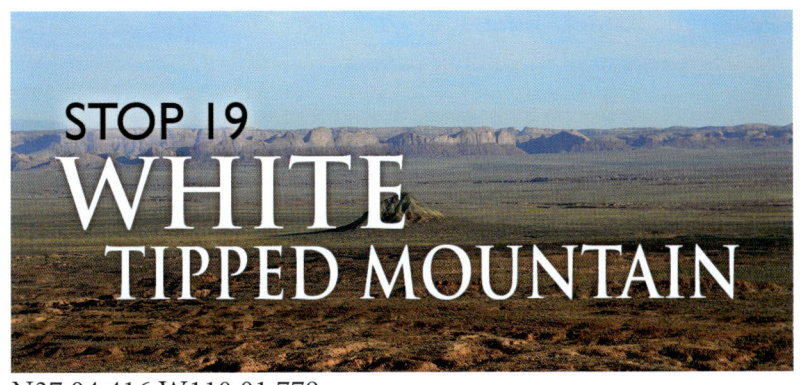

N37 04.416 W110 01.779

Stop Nineteen: White Tipped Mountain: As you look to the east from the road there is a large valley floor in which three drainages flow then meet in Gypsum Creek, approximately three miles north. There is no name for this valley but the drainages are Halgaito (Plain's Water) Wash, Eagle Rock Wash, and Stagecoach Wash. Dry during most of the year, these washes can fill to overflowing during torrential summer rains. Looking south one can see the northern end of Monument Valley's Navajo Tribal Park and pick out certain rock formations such as Totem Pole and Yé'ii Bicheii rocks and Artist's Point. Between Stagecoach and Eagle Rock washes lies a small aptly-named formation called on topographical maps Conical Butte, but to the Navajo is White Tipped Mountain. A Navajo elder raised in this area during the 1920s recalls, "There were a lot of wild mustangs in that wide open space. Each stallion had several mares of a variety of colors; white, beige with black manes, beige and yellow with white manes, black, brown, and reddish brown horses, and spotted ones. Some of these animals belonged to a person named Yellow Man. We gathered these horses and chased them up through the monuments. There were so many of them that they had almost taken up the whole space between the rocks." Occasionally, the people would butcher some for meat while others were tamed for riding. We also used to gather wild mustangs. We'd chase these horses all day long, riding bareback. By the end of the day, our tail bones were rubbed raw and painful. We had to lie almost on our stomachs atop the horse all the way home. There was a man called Thin Yucca Fruit, who loved to chase horses. He did not want to stop, urging us to go again and again. His horse was slow and straggly, but he was proud of it." Horse meat was often eaten in the winter for its medicinal value, believed to prevent colds.

STOP 20
DOUGLAS MESA

N37 04.001 W110 .03.779   and   N37 03.189 W110 05.373

Stop Twenty: Douglas Mesa: After passing the Red Lands Viewpoint with its vendors' booths and proceeding a short distance to the point just before entering Monument Valley, a road to the west serves as the main artery of travel on Douglas Mesa. This approximately twenty-mile-long plateau that ends at the San Juan River near the Goosenecks is the home to many Navajo families who originally settled on this land because of the rich grass available for livestock. This displaced most of the Paiutes living there at the time. Two explanations exist as to how this formation received its Anglo name. The first is that William B. Douglass of the General Land Office, who traveled in this general area during the 1909 expedition to discover Rainbow Bridge at Navajo Mountain, provided the name. The second, and more likely derivation, comes from a miner named James Douglas who prospected on the San Juan River. Disillusioned by good luck that turned sour, he committed suicide by jumping off the bridge at Mexican Hat in 1929, but not before leaving a note. It read: "When this you see, my old body in the river will be. There is no one in the world to blame for this—only me."

The Navajo name for this mesa is Tsé Bił Deez'áhígíí meaning "Mesa Extending Out." Elders speak of all the mesas that align between Douglas Mesa and the Bears Ears forming a pathway walked by the Holy People during their travels. Rock formations, springs, and other sacred sites have their own names and functions. Medicine man John Holiday, born in 1919, shares an experience he had on the southern end of Douglas Mesa when he was twelve years old boy. He was serving as an apprentice to his grandfather, Metal Teeth (Béésh Biwoo'ii), when three men approached them with a request. Through divination—both crystal gazing and hand trembling—the powers directed the three men to their camp, stating that the drought at this time was so bad and the people's suffering so great, that something had to be done or they would all perish. Another medicine man, Black Hair Who Laughs (Ts'ínaajinii Ánádlohí), had already performed a ceremony for several days but without success. Metal Teeth agreed to conduct another rain-making ceremony, but then turned to his grandson and told him that he would be the one to do it. After getting over the shock, John spent the next two days in the sweat lodge and the hogan rehearsing the songs and prayers with his mentor. After procuring the necessary supplies, the two set out for Douglas Mesa and the opportunity for a frightened novice to enter the world of power.

    John starts his account: "As we reached the top of the hill overlooking Mister Red Houses's (Hastiin Kinłich'íí'nii) home, we saw a group of men working on the big summer shelter in which the ceremony would take place. Another large structure stood beside it, where people prepared food and ate. There were many, many visitors—too many—and wagons and horses. The news had gotten around, with travelers coming from Black Mesa, Teec Nos Pos, Lukachukai, and other distant areas. Some had come in the Wagon That Runs Fast (car). The people had already butchered some sheep as a blanket of grill smoke arose from the cooking shelter.

    "When we rode to the men building the large shelter, we saw that one of them was Black Hair Who Laughs, the man who had tried to sing for rain but failed. We noticed that he was putting the shelter trees upside down. They are supposed to be right side up. 'No, no take them all out and set them upright. They grow upwards!' said Grandfather. 'We are going to sing for rain, and those trees are to sit upwards to grow! Black Hair Who Laughs probably did his ceremonies like that, so it is no wonder his rain song failed to work,' Metal Teeth scolded him. Grandfather must have been a great man to have gotten after a medicine man who was knowledgeable. If he saw something being done wrong, he corrected it. He was just that way.

"We brought our medicine bags inside the ceremonial place. There was a young boy and girl sitting inside, who would serve as the Rain Boy and Rain Girl. 'These two will accommodate you in singing and praying for rain,' I was told. I was just as young as they were and was quite nervous. It was a critical time, with all eyes upon me, especially those of the knowledgeable medicine men who had come to observe and take part in the activity. I was led to my seat against the wall of the hogan where my grandfather sat down beside me. I was scared!

"The ceremony began. We performed the prayer and rituals, and the next day, at dawn, everyone took a sweat bath. There were two sweat lodges, one for the women and another for the men. In the men's sweat lodge, the medicine men and the people who sat in as the patients were the first group to go inside. For this ritual, men hauled barrels of water by wagon from Water in Both Directions, near Douglas Mesa. Water from Owl Spring and Salty Water Spring filled a dugout nearby. Both of these sources produced quite a bit of water.

"We crawled inside the hot sweat lodge and sat down. Then, out of nowhere, we heard a frog croaking. 'Shine the light inside, open the blanket door. Let's see where it's coming from! These are the sounds of Female-Rain Girl (Níłtsą́ At'ééd) and Male-Rain Boy (Níłtsą́ Ashkii). There they are, sitting side by side in the farthest corner of the sweat lodge. Catch them and throw them in the puddle outside!' they said. The men caught the two frogs and put them in the puddle. The poor little frogs were taking a sweat bath, too, but were removed and thrown in the water with a splash! We continued our sweat while the frogs croaked in the puddle.

"After the ceremony, I went to the water to wash and did the sacred wash ritual on the young boy and girl. There is actually no particular patient or client, just the two children who assisted, Female-Rain Girl and Male-Rain Boy. After the bath everyone covered themselves with ground-corn powder and spread a large blanket outside for the offerings of sacred stones. This is part of the ritual when the little stone offerings are selected and put together to take to a sacred spot, prayed over, and left. Before we went with these offerings, there was a request made by the men who came from faraway places. They wanted to take some of these sacred stones with them to their homes, because it was not raining there either.

"They also suggested, 'We'll walk and take these offerings to all the water wells in different places around here.' Grandfather said, 'No, I don't do it like that. I place all the sacred stones in one place only.' We took them to one little spot near the mesa where there was a small oasis of water. I said the prayers as we laid down the offerings, speaking to the four sacred points of the earth. While I was doing this, there was a sound of thunder, then another, but there was not a cloud in the sky, and it was very hot. Suddenly a cloud began to form above us, and just as I finished the prayers, it started to rain! The clouds poured forth buckets of water. It was a long way back to the homestead so our handmade moccasins became soaking wet. Streams of water were everywhere, going in every direction. Once we arrived home, we did the one-night Blessing Way. It rained so hard that it snowed, covering the sand dunes with a thick blanket of white moisture. Ribbons of water flowed among the sand dunes as it rained and rained for four days, proving our sacred songs and prayers a success. It was holy."

STOP 21
EAGLE MESA

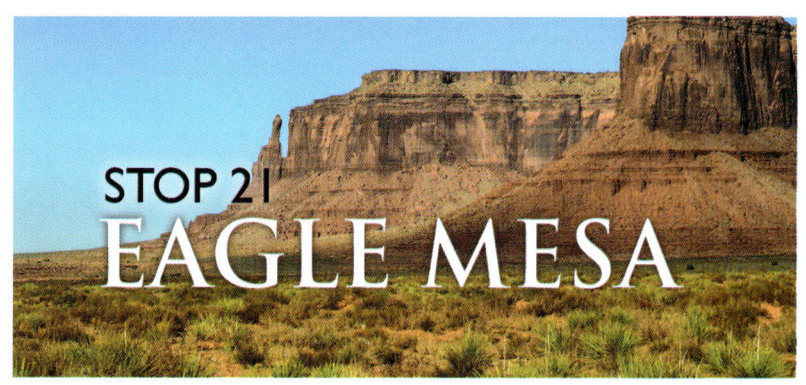

N37 01.245 W110 08.645

Stop Twenty-one: Eagle Mesa and Eagle Rock: As you go up the hill and through Monument Pass, there are spires, mesas, and other rock formations on both sides of the road. Each has a story and name—too many to be handled within the scope of this tour. But to mention a few—on the right hand side (west) and closest to the road is the Setting Hen said to be a turkey frozen in stone. The large mesa next to it is Eagle Rock Mesa, which, as with so many other formations, has more than one name. Some Navajo elders refer to it as Tsé Łichii Dahazkání, meaning "Elevated Red Rock Sitting Up." Others call it "Where the Eagles Roost" because in the past it seemed to attract these birds during the nesting season, while other names include Wide Rock and Trees Hanging from Surrounding Belt because there used to be a lot of vegetation around the mesa. It is also said that the spirit of the dead sometimes go to Eagle Mesa. Standing beside this large formation is a slender pinnacle, Eagle Rock. This spire is most visible when you reach the last bend in the road that leads to the four way intersection where the high school is located. The rock looks like an eagle, perched on a stand, suggesting its name. Navajo names for this rock include Eagle alongside Mesa, Standing Slim Rock Alongside, and Big Finger Is Pointed.

  One elder raised in this area, said: "Eagle Mesa is called Water Basket Sits. People say there is a male hogan on top of it. A while back, when I used to live within view, we used to see moving lights on top. I do not know which direction the lights went down the mesa, and I do not know who it was." Another person confirmed the sighting of moving lights, a phenomenon associated with skinwalkers who separate after holding their witchcraft meeting to go their way to perform evil deeds. The same person, who has since passed away, noted that when he was a boy there was a rope made of yucca fiber that went to the top of the rock which he attributed to the Anasazi. It is no longer there.

STOP 22
MONUMENT VALLEY

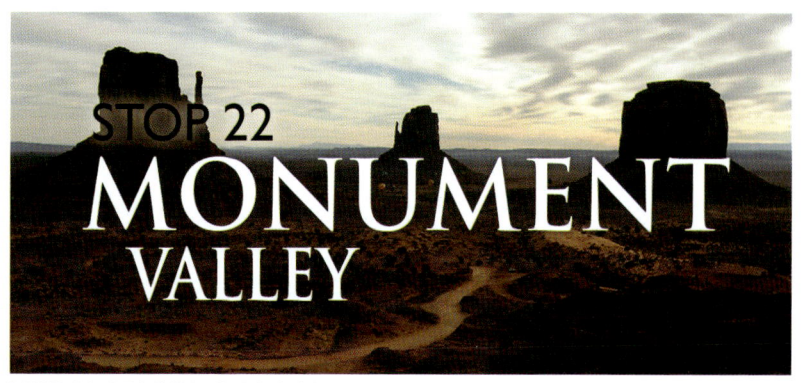

N37 00.159 W110 10.366

Stop Twenty-two: Monument Valley: Our tour ends in Monument Valley proper. The Valley is most famous for the scenery included in the 91,696 acre Navajo Tribal Park dedicated in 1960 whose entrance is located in Utah. The Valley itself extends into Arizona where a good portion of the park is found, but many of the most-photographed rock formations are in the northern end. The western films of John Wayne and John Ford, as well as many more contemporary movies and advertisements, attest to the dramatic scenery and picturesque landscape. As should be apparent by now, each of these rock formations has at least one name, a number of teachings, holds power, and is important to the local Navajo people. For two reasons, most of this will not be discussed here. The first and most obvious reason is that to do justice to these beliefs and shared experience, it would require another tour with extensive information to capture the land's meaning. This leads to the second reason and that is that a number of Navajo families offer such tours and make their livelihood from them. There is no desire to compete against the people whose land this is.

Nevertheless, some brief comments are still in order. The traditional Navajo name for Monument Valley is "White Streaks amid the Rocks" (Tsé Bii' Nidzisgai) or "Clearing among the Rocks" (Tsé Bii' Halgai Hazá). Some elders view the valley as a hogan. Its fireplace is the butte near Goulding's Trading Post while its door faces east near the Tribal Park ranger station, Sentinel Mesa and Gray Whiskers Mesa being the door posts. At Gray Whiskers Mesa, Eagle Mesa, and Mitchell Butte are water seeps at which earth bundles and prayers are offered. Many of these formations are also viewed as water barrels.

There are entire books written on the history and culture of the people living in Monument Valley and so perhaps the best thing to do is to close with a concern expressed by two of the Valley's inhabitants. Each year including 2012, the park averages 263,000 visitors, give or take one or two. Tourism is an important part of the local economy but at the same time, families have their homes here, local people are caught up in their daily life, and the landscape of a desert environment is extremely fragile with intrusions not easily erased. What emerges from this are two perspectives. One person noted: "Many receive lots of money. When a bus stops tourists come to buy many of the items the people are selling. . . . This is what they do, the ones who put their things in the sun." Others feel the money is going to the tribal government in Window Rock and hope that it will return to them through chapter (local government) funds. However there are others who are concerned about the sheer volume of people. As one man put it, "The Anglos just flock and stream in the area. I do not know how to slow this down. Now they are crawling all over behind our back. There is no hope." As you enter and explore Monument Valley and take an opportunity to get out of the car and stretch, enjoy the view but remember the people.

This concludes our car tour over Highway 163 from Bluff to Monument Valley. Hopefully everyone involved recognizes the importance of the land to the Navajo people.

What might just be a rock or river or abandoned site holds power, provides teachings, evokes memories, offers assistance, and preserves culture. These elements are fundamental to Navajo thought and future cultural persistence. Given the intensity of learning that you have experienced just by driving along this route, consider multiplying it over the 27,425 square miles of the reservation contained within southeastern Utah, northeastern Arizona, and northwestern New Mexico, not to mention other elements that are not directly on the reservation. One can see the rich body of knowledge available for teaching and religious practice, yet preservation of this knowledge is a real concern. As elders pass away, so does much of the instruction fundamental to this way of life. Appreciation for what they have shared will hopefully make us all better people.

Photos by Kay Shumway

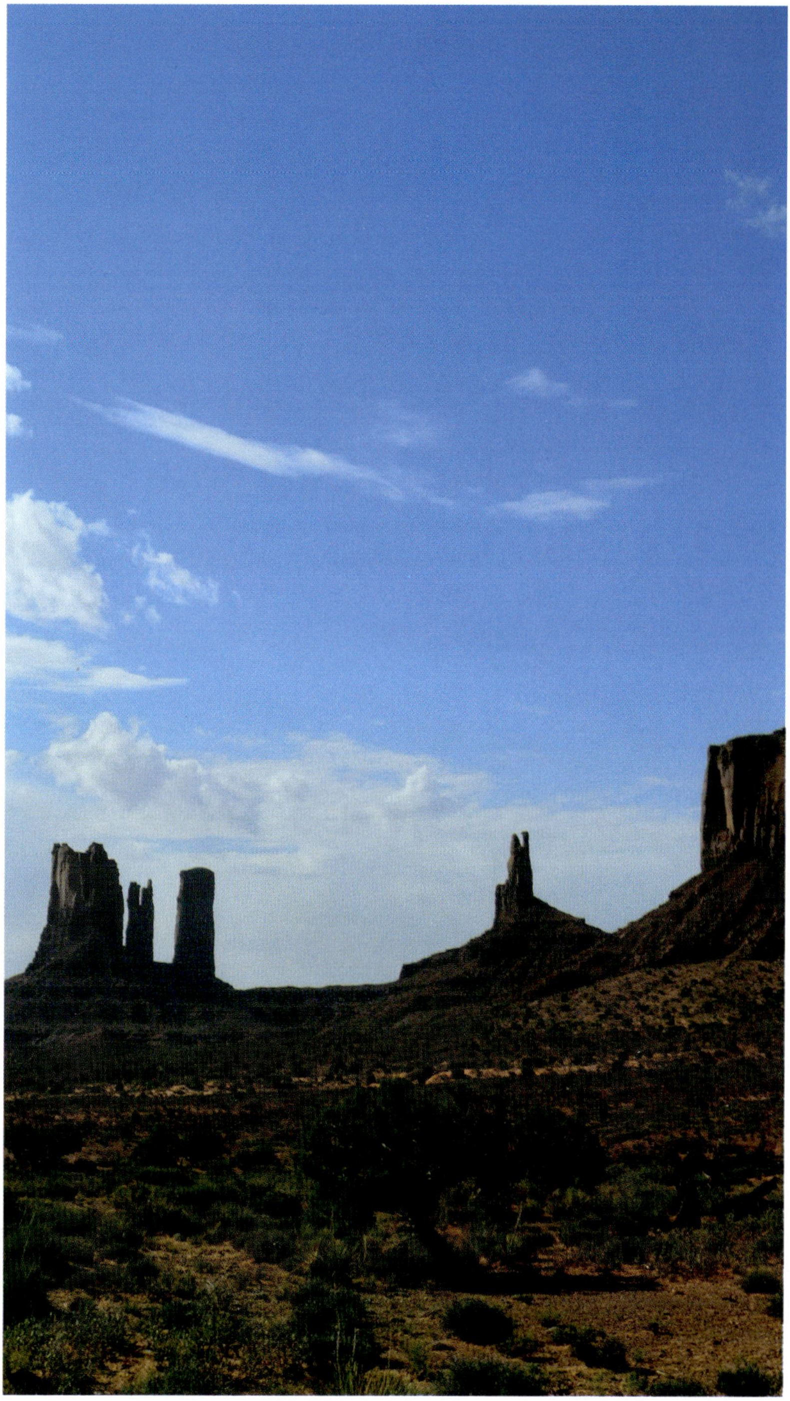

Trip Notes